Cambridge Elements

Elements in Contentious Politics
edited by
David S. Meyer
University of California, Irvine
Suzanne Staggenborg
University of Pittsburgh

THE CONTENTIOUS POLITICS OF GLOBAL HEALTH MOVEMENTS

Contesting Patents in Pandemic Times

Donatella della Porta
Scuola Normale Superiore, Florence

Stella Christou
Scuola Normale Superiore, Florence

Shaftesbury Road, Cambridge CB2 8EA, United Kingdom

One Liberty Plaza, 20th Floor, New York, NY 10006, USA

477 Williamstown Road, Port Melbourne, VIC 3207, Australia

314–321, 3rd Floor, Plot 3, Splendor Forum, Jasola District Centre, New Delhi – 110025, India

103 Penang Road, #05–06/07, Visioncrest Commercial, Singapore 238467

Cambridge University Press is part of Cambridge University Press & Assessment, a department of the University of Cambridge.

We share the University's mission to contribute to society through the pursuit of education, learning and research at the highest international levels of excellence.

www.cambridge.org
Information on this title: www.cambridge.org/9781009658607
DOI: 10.1017/9781009658591

© Donatella della Porta and Stella Christou 2025

This publication is in copyright. Subject to statutory exception and to the provisions of relevant collective licensing agreements, no reproduction of any part may take place without the written permission of Cambridge University Press & Assessment.

When citing this work, please include a reference to the DOI 10.1017/9781009658591

First published 2025

A catalogue record for this publication is available from the British Library

ISBN 978-1-009-65860-7 Hardback
ISBN 978-1-009-65862-1 Paperback
ISSN 2633-3570 (online)
ISSN 2633-3562 (print)

Cambridge University Press & Assessment has no responsibility for the persistence or accuracy of URLs for external or third-party internet websites referred to in this publication and does not guarantee that any content on such websites is, or will remain, accurate or appropriate.

For EU product safety concerns, contact us at Calle de José Abascal, 56, 1°, 28003 Madrid, Spain, or email eugpsr@cambridge.org

The Contentious Politics of Global Health Movements
Contesting Patents in Pandemic Times

Elements in Contentious Politics

DOI: 10.1017/9781009658591
First published online: November 2025

Donatella della Porta
Scuola Normale Superiore, Florence

Stella Christou
Scuola Normale Superiore, Florence

Author for correspondence: Donatella della Porta,
Donatella.dellaporta@sns.it

Abstract: While much research has addressed the regressive anti-vax protests, this Element focuses on campaigns by progressive social movements to promote the development of vaccines for Covid-19 and ensure their equal access on a global level. Over the course of the pandemic, health and care have become central claims, mobilising health workers and patients as well as citizens in general. Together with various local and national social movement organisations which converged on health rights, through the use of care and cure as bridging frames, transnational campaigns addressing patents on vaccines also unfolded. This Element analyses these transnational campaigns, with particular attention to their organisational models, repertoires of action and collective framing. It assesses their outcomes by considering the complex sets of opportunities and constraints that the Covid-19 pandemic presented for progressive social movements that fight for access to medicines and cures at a global level.

Keywords: transnational movements, health social movements, Covid-19, vaccines, public health

© Donatella della Porta and Stella Christou 2025

ISBNs: 9781009658607 (HB), 9781009658621 (PB), 9781009658591 (OC)
ISSNs: 2633-3570 (online), 2633-3562 (print)

Contents

1 Health Rights and Social Movements: An Introduction   1

2 The Patent System and the Fight for Access to Medicines   11

3 The 'No Profit on Pandemic' Initiative in the EU   25

4 Mobilising for Universal Access to Covid-19 Vaccines: The Campaign in Support of India and South Africa's Patent Waiver Proposal   40

5 Transnational Protests for Access to Medicines: Some Conclusions   56

List of Abbreviations   62

List of Interviews Cited   63

References   64

1 Health Rights and Social Movements: An Introduction

While much research on the Covid-19 pandemic has focused on collective action against Covid-19 vaccinations, less attention has been paid to struggles aimed at defending and promoting the right to health (but see Carpiano et al., 2023; della Porta, 2023; Mylan & Hardman, 2021; Venizelos & Trimithiotis, 2024). Over the course of the pandemic, health and healthcare emerged as key demands put forward by social movements, mobilising health workers, patients and citizens. In general, the contentious politics of health rights have addressed issues relating to the public provision of healthcare, environmental health, the social determinants of health, occupational health and safety, and the neoliberalisation of the health system. The pandemic also sparked debates about medical power and biopolitical control, fuelling demands for the democratisation of decision-making within health systems and for universal and free access to health services. Building on earlier traditions of health movements, the pandemic elevated the right to health to a dominant frame, linking existing collective actors with newly constituted ones with the aim of addressing the immediate pressures of the health emergency while envisioning future alternatives. While social movement organisations at the local and national levels converged on the right to health, using care and healing as a bridging frame, at the transnational level campaigns were developed around patents on vaccines.

This Element focuses on two major campaigns that sought to ensure equal distribution and free access to Covid-19 vaccines. Considering these campaigns as examples of contestations of global health politics, we will analyse their organisational models, repertoires of action and collective framing, while also assessing their outcomes within the complex set of opportunities and constraints that the Covid-19 pandemic presented for social movements mobilising for access to vaccines.

In what follows, we will present these transnational campaigns against patents on the Covid-19 vaccines as part of the broader tradition of Health Social Movements (HSMs) (Brown & Zavestoski, 2004). Having conceptualised Health Social Movements as a distinct category of social movements, the section will briefly introduce some of the key characteristics that define these movements in terms of their multiple repertoires of contention, broad and fragmented organisational coalitions, and diagnostic and prognostic frames. Highlighting the global dimension in the definition and defence of health rights, the section will identify opportunities and constraints for transnational social movement campaigns. The section will conclude with a brief presentation of the selected case studies, the research methods and sources used, followed by an overview of the volume.

Conceptualising Health Social Movements

Health Social Movements (HSMs) have been conceptualised as a distinct category of social movements, defined as 'collective campaigns to bring about change in medical and public health policy, beliefs, research and practice' (Taylor & Zald, 2013: 550; see also Brown & Zavestoski, 2004). HSMs often challenge stereotypes about the genetic, physiological and psychological origins of health and illness, questioning their causal relationships and exposing their social, political and cultural determinants and implications (Banaszak-Holl et al., 2010; Christou, 2022a; Taylor & Zald, 2000).

While social movement studies have sporadically examined health-related movements, research has revealed the fact that they are not only largely heterogeneous but also greatly fragmented in terms of their organisational structures. Waves of protest have developed broad critiques of mainstream medicine as well as specific diagnostic categories and curative practices associated with particular conditions. HSMs have targeted public health institutions as well as pharmaceutical companies and other commercial, yet relevant, actors. From an organisational perspective, this fragmentation of protest along the various dimensions of health highlights the relevance of coalition building for HSMs, but also related challenges (Epstein, 2010; Taylor & Zald, 2013).

This fragmentation is evident in the diverse repertoires of action, shaped by the social and political backgrounds of the claimants and the decision-making levels they target. Examples of this heterogeneous set of contentious forms include strikes launched by the labour movement involved in the health sector (Galanti & Naughton, 2023), direct action tactics by environmentalists (Brown, 2007), awareness-raising and self-help within feminist milieus (Barone, 2024) and civil disobedience undertaken by the gay and lesbian movement(s) of the 1980s and 1990s (Stockdill, 2013), to name but a few. More generally, HSMs aim to raise awareness and/or challenge experts through cultural events and communication campaigns, put pressure on public institutions through marches, petitions and lobbying, target pharmaceutical companies and public figures through naming and shaming campaigns, and often use legal strategies to challenge opponents in court. Tactics of self-help and mutualism have proliferated at the local level, more disruptive protest campaigns have targeted the national level, while insider strategies have dominated the transnational level. In general, Health Social Movements have been more visible on the streets when health crises have hit hard, as in the case of the HIV/AIDS pandemic.

Framing is also key for health movements, as they use powerful justice and rights frames. Given the fact that these movements need to address the stifling effects of certain grievances and sentiments – similar to those related to disease or extreme poverty (Gonzales Santos 2024) – they need to develop cognitive and emotional strategies that are capable of translating individual experiences into political grievances, destigmatising collective identities and mobilising affected constituencies (Christou, 2022a). As such, health movements have been instrumental in the development of our health systems, advancing health rights, shaping curative practices and influencing research agendas and diagnostic categories. This has implications for the framing processes they employ and the outcomes they achieve, as

> [c]ollective subjects can be created in the name of health .... Health movements often disrupt stereotypes about the genetic, physiological and psychological origins of health and disease, questioning their causal relationships and exposing their social, political and cultural determinants and implications. They actively create new associations from existing assemblages, effectively transforming the private experience of illness into a public issue. (Christou, 2022a: 2)

In doing so, HSMs respond to specific challenges and opportunities related to the structural and cultural characteristics of the health arena, as activists must navigate both state paternalism and the commodification of health within the market. In addition, HSMs are shaped and constrained by a specific material health infrastructure and an immaterial bioethical-legal framework (Christou, 2022b).

Health Movements, Health Systems and Health Rights

Health Social Movements have not only confronted, but also influenced, practices and conceptions relating to health and medicine. They have not only challenged medical science as the 'dominant epidemiological paradigm' (Brown et al., 2012: 24) but also informed it from its earliest steps. They have also been central to the co-development of our health systems and the current human and health rights frameworks as we know them today.

As early as the nineteenth century, social reformers, urban planners and physicians mobilised against the unhygienic living conditions of the urban poor, which often triggered deadly epidemics like cholera, linked to rapid urbanisation (Winslow, 1943). Efforts to contain contagion led to identifying 'filth' as a disease carrier – an idea that predated germ theory and laid the groundwork for public health agencies focused on disease prevention through social reform (Singer, 2009). Alongside these developments, experts advanced more holistic views of health, tracing disease to socio-economic conditions rooted in capitalism (Hamlin & Jones, 1998; Waitzkin, 1981). These insights informed early demands for universal rights to a 'healthful existence' (Engels,

2009), forming the basis of modern epidemiology and the socio-economic rights central to contemporary public and global health (Gaffney, 2018).

In the nineteenth and twentieth centuries, grassroots movements also developed claims to health. The emergent labour movement mobilised for health and safety in the workplace and, when successful, influenced paradigmatic industrial reform (Satre, 1982). In Europe, the emergence and consolidation of the working class and its representatives led to the establishment of public health systems, themselves either a product of direct labour victories or of necessary compromises aimed at appeasing class conflict (Gaffney, 2018; Webster, 2002).

Despite the progress marked by these political developments, in terms of both health outcomes and healthcare infrastructure, the Spanish flu pandemic that spread across the globe in the aftermath of the First World War further challenged the strained state of both the healthcare system and society as a whole. Combined with food shortages and unemployment, the Spanish flu triggered intense collective responses, sometimes leading to revolutionary moments. Official responses to the Spanish flu built on the momentum of a growing reform movement and included the introduction of public health services and the centralisation of public health administration. Such was the impact of the flu on the configuration of health systems that historians claim that 'the epidemic was a better campaigner for reform than any politician's speech' (Jenkins, 2007: 337).

The end of the Second World War, on the other hand, ushered in a new era of global governance, including in the field of health. Not coincidentally, at its inception, the United Nations (UN) voted to create an international health organisation to promote global cooperation in the name of public health (Cueto et al., 2019). With this mandate, the World Health Organization (WHO) has promoted a transformative vision of public health, asserting that 'the highest attainable standard of health' is 'one of the fundamental rights of every human being' (WHO, 1948).

Although it was linked to the traditions outlined earlier, this rights-based approach went beyond traditional medicine, proposing a broader definition of health as 'a state of complete physical, mental and social well-being and not merely the absence of disease or infirmity' (ibid.). This definition subsequently structured the WHO's social medicine and reform agenda, which emphasised that '[g]overnments have a responsibility for the health of their people which can only be discharged by the provision of adequate health and social services' (ibid.).

Building on these definitions laid out by the WHO, the UN also included the right to health in its Universal Declaration of Human Rights, stating that

> Everyone has the right to a standard of living adequate for the health and well-being of himself and of his family, including food, clothing, housing and medical care and necessary social services, and the right to security in the event of unemployment, sickness, disability, widowhood, old age or other lack of livelihood in circumstances beyond his control. (United Nations, 1948)

Thus, while the WHO sought to broaden the definition of health to link it to human rights, the UN sought to outline health rights through the multiple and complex determinants of health and universalise them as human rights. The definitions and links established by the two international organisations have had a significant impact on human rights over the past century. They have influenced international law and provided a conceptual framework and benchmark for international non-governmental organisations (NGOs), civil society and social movements to mobilise in their defence and promotion.

These health rights' claims would also be taken up by HSMs and NGOs intervening in health, even as they themselves were undergoing significant changes in line with broader socio-political trends. More specifically, during the 1960s, HSMs acquired the characteristics of what have been termed New Social Movements (Melucci, 1985). Notable examples of this shift include the women's movement's critique of medical and health systems as male-dominated and ultimately sexist, and collective resistance in the name of women's rights (Bracke, 2017; Maraboutaki, 2021) as well as the anti-psychiatry movement, which united medical professionals and patients against the dominant psychiatric logic and practice in Europe and the United States (see Crossley, 2006).

The definition and establishment of health rights paved the way for the WHO's Alma-Ata Declaration in 1978. Alma-Ata brought health equity to the forefront of the international political agenda and established primary healthcare as central to achieving the WHO's goal of 'health for all by the year 2000' (Litsios, 2015). According to Halfdan Mahler, then Director-General of the WHO,

> [h]ealth for all means bringing health within reach of everyone in a given country. And 'health' means a personal state of well-being, not just the availability of health services – a state of health that enables a person to lead a socially and economically productive life. 'Health for all' implies the removal of barriers to health – the elimination of malnutrition, ignorance, contaminated drinking water and unhygienic housing – as well as the solution of purely medical problems such as a shortage of doctors, hospital beds, drugs and vaccines. (Mahler, [1981] 2000)

Concerns about access to diagnostics, vaccines and therapeutics, as discussed in this Element, are thus intimately linked to the advent global health governance and were first articulated in the context of the Health for All campaign. The failure to meet the campaign's agenda by 2000 led to the creation of the Peoples' Health Movement in the same year, which has become the most important civil society network in global health policy, and a defender of access to medicines (Narayan et al., 2020). These concerns gained centrality with the spread of the HIV/AIDS pandemic in the 1980s, and even more so after the signing of the World Trade Organization (WTO) Agreement on Trade-Related Aspects of Intellectual Property Rights (TRIPS) in 1995, which aimed to standardise and harmonise intellectual property rights across sectors and countries.

HIV/AIDS activism evolved in two key phases: the first aimed to destigmatise the virus and affected communities while advancing research, and the second, following the TRIPS agreement, shifted focus to access to new therapies hindered by patents. In the Global North, this activism was largely driven by the LGBT community (Epstein, 1996; Graf, 1992; Stockdill, 2013), whereas in the Global South, it involved a broader coalition of affected communities, the poor and international health and human rights NGOs (Biehl, 2007; Ferraz, 2021; Heywood, 2009). This later phase gave rise to the Access to Medicines (A2M) movement – a loose network of Civil Society Organisations (CSOs), activists, legal scholars and health experts advocating against restrictive intellectual property (IP) rights in the name of health equity. Over three decades, A2 M has collaborated with governments, global institutions and generic drug manufacturers to lower medicine costs in Low- and middle-income countries (LMICs), beginning with HIV/AIDS and expanding to other global health areas.

While issues of access to lifesaving products and technologies dominated much of the global health agenda in the 1990s and 2000s, the global financial crisis of 2008 spurred contestation in a new direction, targeting 'health system neoliberalism' (Gaffney & Muntaner, 2018). This has been defined as the depletion and privatisation of the health system, and the shift in focus from primary prevention to the more profitable secondary and tertiary levels of care. As a consequence, anti-austerity HSMs have often combined protest tactics in support of public ownership and provision of healthcare, improving working conditions in the sector, and protecting and improving the quality of the services it provides, with direct social actions (Bosi & Zamponi, 2015) of healthcare and/or pharmaceutical provision. These campaigns often involved collaboration between healthcare workers and users behind defensive and/or propositional strategies in the name of better health for all (Christou, 2022b; Galanti & Naughton, 2023; People's Health Movement, 2014).

In sum, Health Social Movements have been involved in dynamic and transformative interactions with medical science, health systems, curative practices, diagnostic categories, biomedical and pharmaceutical innovations,

The Covid-19 Global Critical Juncture and Its Discontents

and have been consequential in the development of international health and human rights frameworks.

As shown earlier, epidemics and pandemics have often triggered health rights mobilisations and changed the field of opportunities and challenges in which HSMs operate. This was also the case with the Covid-19 pandemic, as health and care were advanced as central demands, mobilising health workers, patients and citizens more broadly (Christou, 2024; della Porta & Lavizzari, 2022). Indeed, as we will show in the rest of this Element, the pandemic provided an opportunity for the (re)mobilisation of A2M. Building on earlier traditions of Health Social Movements, the pandemic juncture not only remobilised constituencies and milieus active in the defence of health rights, but also had an impact beyond such groups, drawing broader social movement milieus behind the health rights' framework (Christou, 2024; della Porta, 2022; della Porta & Lavizzari, 2022). A broad reference to care was linked to the importance of public health services, with the recognition of the indispensability of care workers, but also to forms of care that became part of our everyday lives during the pandemic, as well as to forms of mutual aid and solidarity networks (della Porta, 2022). In what follows, we will discuss how the Covid-19 pandemic represented a critical juncture for health movements in general and for A2M activism in particular, providing discursive opportunities to challenge the existing and long-contested system of patents for health-related products and technologies (Collier & Munck, 2017; della Porta, 2022). The global dimension of the challenge, together with the unequal distribution of the costs of the pandemic – both within and between countries – gave rise to hopes of global solidarity and commitments to shared solutions.

These hopes and commitments on the part of world leaders became important resources for the remobilisation of A2M and the expansion of its audience. Although A2M focused on vaccines as the primary and most important tool to contain the spread of Covid-19, it used the critical juncture of the pandemic to advance broader critiques of the patent regime, including the system of knowledge production and appropriation, the public funding of private profiteering, and of course the socio-economic and global inequalities that affect access to medicines.

As we will show, the links between the evolution of HSM campaigns at the transnational level during the HIV/AIDS and Covid-19 pandemics are evident in the networks mobilised, the core strategies employed and the collective framing employed, building on the right to health. Despite the virological and epidemiological differences between the two pandemics, they brought about opportunities (and threats) for global mobilisation and cooperation in the name of health. Given the global nature of health challenges, the protest campaigns are often characterised by an upward scale shift (on the concept, see Tarrow and McAdam 2005), targeting big corporations and international governmental organisations that, in this like in other policy areas, increased their regulatory competences but not their democratic accountability, triggering a parallel growth of a global civic society as well as transnational protests (Boli & Thomas 1999; della Porta et al., 1999; della Porta & Tarrow 2005; Smith et al., 1996). Different international institutions offered distinctive opportunities to social movements, that often engaged transnationally in the attempt to change domestic policies through so-called 'boomerang effects' as social movements sought international-level allies to put pressure on domestic institutions (Keck & Sikkink, 1998) through insiders strategies but also open contestations, as in the case of the counter summits of the Global Justice Movement, for which health rights were already central (della Porta et al., 2006).

Similarly to the HIV/AIDS pandemic, Covid-19 acted as an 'emergency critical juncture', bringing the right to health back to the fore and reintroducing debates on the social determinants of health, disease, environmental health, public health and primary care. What is more, the Covid-19 pandemic gave rise to calls for scientific democratisation and transparency, and to struggles against state arbitrage and control. Finally, the pandemic reopened and publicised the debate on medical and scientific knowledge and advanced existing critiques of the appropriate role of the public and private (i.e. pharmaceutical) sectors in it, especially with regards to vaccines for Covid-19 (see della Porta et al., 2024).

As the pandemic was a global challenge, the demand for access to medicines required mobilisation on a global scale. We therefore trace A2M activism at this critical juncture by analysing two transnational contentious campaigns during this period of emergency (della Porta & Tarrow 2005; della Porta 2022). As the campaigns against patents for Covid-19-related products, innovations and therapeutics addressed multilevel targets and constituencies, the analysis of the patent system and its discontents provides a lens through which to study health rights protests at the national, transnational and international levels.

Moreover, given that several international organisations are involved, this analysis allows us highlight the specific opportunities and threats posed by organisations as diverse as the WTO, the WHO and the EU. In addition, the fact that these major campaigns against patents on health-related products developed in times of emergency further reinforces the relevance of critical junctures for social movement studies. By looking at transnational campaigns, we address the ways in which multilevel contestation affects their repertoires of action, forms of organisation and collective frames. We also reflect on the outcomes of these organised efforts, contextualising them within the broader history of patent contestation and health movements more broadly.

Given the nature of the challenges they face, HSMs often involve the transnationalisation of contentious collective action. In particular, during the HIV/AIDS and Covid-19 pandemics, global mobilisation for the right to health unfolded, shifting scale from the local to the international level. By highlighting the deadly effects of unequal access to public healthcare within and between countries and regions, research on the contested politics of health during the two pandemics allows us to explore similarities and differences that exist in the way movements act, organise and formulate their strategic goals in distinct contexts.

As we shall see, while some of their attempts to transform the international regime towards health rights have been successful, interactions with particularly closed international organisations such as the WTO – but also with relatively more open UN-related international organisations such as the WHO – have pushed transnational organisations towards moderating their goals, seeking achievements within the existing normative system while privileging insider strategies and organisational structuring. However, this trend has at times been challenged during more visible health challenges, including the HIV/AIDS pandemic, when transnational efforts were supported by grassroots organisations using more disruptive tactics and radical frames against the commodification of health and neoliberal capitalism. Our analysis will, therefore, explore continuities as well as discontinuities in the transnational struggle for health rights. In doing so, we will look at the transformative power of protests not only in terms of policy change but also in terms of the accumulation of organisational resources and experience (della Porta, 2020).

The Research and This Element

In this Element, we will analyse two transnational A2M campaigns that developed over the course of the Covid-19 pandemic. The first of these revolved around a European Citizens' Initiative (ECI) targeting the European Commission under the banner 'No Profit on Pandemic'. The campaign aimed at the ECI, which failed to reach the required number of signatures, was mobilised on behalf of existing A2M networks in Europe, including grassroots social movement organisations and more structured CSOs. The second campaign was launched in support of the patent waiver proposal put forward to the WTO by India and South Africa. The waiver campaign, which involved the backbone of A2M activism, had an unprecedented reach, opening up the debate on intellectual property rights to – until then – distant milieus and fora. As a result of the pressure placed on them by the mobilisation, the WTO adopted a compromise solution, with the aim of achieving a multi-country supported patent waiver.

Our empirical analysis is based on thirty in-depth interviews with activists involved in transnational campaigns for access to medicines at different territorial levels. In addition, we analysed over 100 documents issued by the coordinating committees and main organisations involved in these campaigns, and drew on our participant observation of two transnational meetings related to these campaigns. Secondary analysis of the existing literature helped us to reconstruct the contextual opportunities and threats that arose during the Covid-19 pandemic, the historical development and consolidation of the patent system, and the collective responses to this regime.

Before looking at the campaigns themselves, Section 2 will present the contested politics of patents as they developed in interaction with the mobilisations of Access to Medicines (A2M) and other health movements. Throughout its three-decade history, A2M has worked with national governments, international health institutions and generic medicine manufacturers to achieve significant reductions in the price of medicines for specific diseases in LMICs, thereby ensuring wider access to medicines and, more broadly, to health. A2M was itself the product of collective concerns and responses to the WTO's TRIPS Agreement, signed in 1995. This section thus sets the scene for the analysis of patent contestation over the course of the Covid-19 pandemic by introducing the evolution of the patent system, highlighting the ways in which movements have influenced WTO rules, pointing to their (limited) successes, and outlining the long-term challenges that have emerged for future mobilisations.

Section 3 focuses on the 'No Profit on Pandemic' European Citizens' Initiative and examines the ways in which the pandemic influenced contentious politics directed at EU institutions. In particular, the section examines the campaign's repertoires of action, organisational networks and collective framing, as well as its short-term outcomes. The analysis shows that, at least in its early stages, the pandemic was perceived by social movement organisations as a discursive opportunity to improve access to medicines. However, the campaign faced significant challenges. Specifically, in terms of the repertoire of action, the campaign had to face the constraining effects of the pandemic, but also the limitations and obstacles inherent in the use of the European Citizens' Initiative. In terms of organisational resources, activists point to the difficulties of coordination between the national, European and global levels, as well as the legacy of previous divisions within the A2M movement. In terms of collective framing, the campaigns had to deal with tensions arising from the definition of the pandemic as an emergency requiring ad hoc solutions in a largely uncontested patent system. Finally, Europe's position within the global pharmaceutical industry strengthened the alliance between the European Commission and the large pharmaceutical companies, splitting the movement into different strategic agendas.

Building on the previous section, Section 4 focuses on the international campaign for a patent waiver during the Covid-19 pandemic. In October 2020, in the midst of international negotiations on vaccines and growing concerns about the impact of these negotiations on LMICs, India and South Africa submitted a radical proposal to the WTO calling for a patent waiver. The two countries were later joined by around one hundred others in calling for the removal of patents and their licensing for national production of Covid-related vaccines, diagnostics and therapeutics. The proposal built on the WHO and WTO's characterisation of the pandemic as 'exceptional' and 'unprecedented' and their respective calls for global solidarity. In addition, the campaign highlighted the 'disproportionate' impact of the virus in LMICs, both economically and in terms of health outcomes. In light of this, the campaign called for the abandonment of patent laws for these products and the scaling-up of production on a global scale. The proposal was supported by some 300 institutions and CSOs, organised as part of a transnational coalition. The campaign was partially successful, although the waiver was late in being applied and included many restrictions. As in the previous section, the focus is on the campaign's repertoires of action, organisational networks and collective framing, highlighting the opportunities and challenges associated with this mobilisation.

Finally, Section 5 summarises the empirical findings presented in the previous three sections by returning to the main theoretical issues raised in the introduction. Looking at the broader opportunities and challenges for health movements mobilising at the global level, we will highlight the specific strategies available to transnational coalitions fighting for global access to medicines and healthcare, including the dilemmas faced by social movement organisations.

2 The Patent System and the Fight for Access to Medicines

The transnational campaigns of the right to health movement have focused on the evolution of the patent regime for health-related technologies, innovations and products, considering its impact on access to medicines worldwide. The mobilisation in the name of equal access to essential medicines has particularly targeted those international organisations that have the most influence on these issues, namely the World Trade Organization and the World Health Organization – the former being seen as the main opponent, with the latter considered a potential ally. As we will see in this section, the evolution of the patent regime has been influenced by multilevel mobilisations that combine the lobbying of more structured CSOs at the international level with the more disruptive repertoires of grassroots activists at the national level. While campaigns have on occasion been able to combine the efforts of both approaches, divisions have emerged not only in terms of forms of action and organisational models, but also in relation to the very framing of the struggle. In what follows, we will present an outline of the chronology of these developments, looking at the main challenges that Access to Medicines has had to face and the ways in which it has responded to them.

The Origins of the Patent System

Health-related patents have been at the centre of scientific and political debate since they were first applied in the United States and Europe in the eighteenth and nineteenth centuries. In both contexts, lawmakers, medical practitioners and scientists alike were concerned about the balance between IP rights, the public good and the advancement of public knowledge. Indeed, the tensions inherent in IP rights fuelled collective reactions to patents, leading to a series of patent laws, amendments and reversals over the years.

Early examples of such reactions include the American Medical Association's explicit condemnation of the use of patents by scientists and physicians in its 1847 Code of Ethics, which stated that 'for a physician to hold a patent for any surgical instrument or medicine' was 'derogatory to [their] professional character' (in Swann, 1988). At the same time, during the same period French authorities were extending patents to all products as a way of regulating and ensuring their public ownership and use (see Cassier, 2014 for more details).

Despite these tensions, or perhaps because of them, historians see health-related patents as key to the development of biomedical science, the medical profession and contemporary health institutions and regulatory bodies (Gaudillière, 2008). Indeed, scholars have argued that early patenting efforts were driven by a 'public good' ethos, as patents served to differentiate 'scientific' products from non-scientific remedies while ensuring that they remained in the hands of public institutions, namely universities.

Over the course of the twentieth century, the industrialisation of the pharmaceutical industry and the associated acceleration of both research and development (R&D) and clinical trials led to a sharp increase in the number of patent applications for new drugs and products. This multiplication of applications corresponded to a radical shift in the relationship between patents and the public good, as patents were reframed as necessary incentives for innovation that ultimately promoted the public good (Cameron & Berger, 2005). Even then, however, the patent system was neither as universal nor as rigid as it is today, as the appropriateness and applicability of patents were configured around the 'trade-off between dynamic benefits (incentives to innovate) and static costs (higher prices, reduced access)' (Shadlen et al., 2020: 77).

In an attempt to balance these concerns, patents were declared inapplicable in LMICs because their costs were considered too high and their benefits too low for scientific and pharmaceutical innovation (Chin & Grossman, 1988). In addition to this, in the 1970s, countries such as Brazil and India took pharmaceutical products off patents altogether and invested in infrastructure to develop generic alternatives to some foreign-made drugs. Finally, on a number of occasions individual patents were revoked for reasons pertaining to public health and/or banned for whole classes of drugs where the drugs in question and the conditions they were meant to cure were considered ambiguous and ill-defined (Cassier, 2004; Gaudillière, 2008; MacLeod, 1988; Mowery & Sampat, 2001).

To date, scholars in both medicine and law have fundamentally challenged the assumption that patents trigger innovation. Informed critiques of the patent regime go beyond the question of access to medicines, arguing that patents distort the research agenda in more profitable directions at the expense of the public good. Furthermore, the same scholars highlight the stagnation of knowledge production over the years, as patents jeopardise the dissemination and use of knowledge (Cameron & Berger, 2005; Gøtzsche, 2018; Sellin, 2015; Shadlen et al., 2020). As we will see next, these tensions and associated critiques would only multiply and intensify following the signing of the TRIPS Agreement.

TRIPS and the Internationalisation of Patents

This slow and controversial evolution of the patent regime underwent a radical change in 1995 with the WTO's Trade-Related Aspects of Intellectual Property (TRIPS) Agreement, which sought to streamline and 'harmonise' intellectual property law across sectors and throughout the world, extending it beyond rich nations (Shadlen et al., 2020). In a nutshell, TRIPS requires all WTO member states to (1) provide for a minimum 20-year period of exclusive patent ownership by the patent holder, (2) patent both products and processes, and (3) protect test data from competition. Given the historical contestation of patents, this geographical extension of IP rights can be seen as a victory for pharmaceutical companies and their lobbyists (Drahos, 1995, 2021; Shadlen et al., 2020).

The TRIPS agreement came with 'safeguards', that is, flexibilities, for countries wishing to challenge individual patents in the name of public health and the wider public good. In the area of health-related innovations, these flexibilities consisted of two main strategies: Compulsory Licensing[1] and Parallel Importation.[2] However, these flexibilities are difficult to implement as they require lengthy legal procedures and expertise. Even when they can be implemented, they are usually challenged by the vested interests of pharmaceutical companies and lobbies. This explains why national governments have rarely sought flexibilities since the signing of the TRIPS Agreement.

The historical context in which the TRIPS Agreement was signed was particularly important for the development of collective litigation against health-related patents. In the mid-1990s, the world was still reeling from the shock of the HIV/AIDS pandemic. The globalisation of pharmaceutical IP rights and their concomitant strengthening thus raised fears about the growing disparities between the Global North and the Global South, as well as concerns about access to treatment for those most affected by the pandemic, that is, the world's poorest.

Relatedly, the TRIPS agreement has also fuelled fears about the future of innovation and the fossilisation of the research agenda around expensive treatments that can only be afforded by wealthy nations. According to the WHO Commission on Intellectual Property Rights, Innovation and Public Health (2006)

> [b]etween 1975 and 2004, of the 1556 new chemical entities marketed worldwide, only 20 (1.3%) were new drugs for tropical diseases and tuberculosis, diseases that account for 12% of the total disease burden. There is no evidence that the implementation of the TRIPS Agreement in developing countries will significantly increase R&D for drugs for type II[3] and especially type III diseases[4]. Insufficient market incentives are the key factor. (ibid.: 85)

In response to these critiques and concerns over the course of the HIV/AIDS pandemic, the Access to Medicines (A2M) movement emerged as a coalition of CSOs, activists, legal scholars and global health experts to advocate for the right to health by challenging IP rights on health-related products such as

---

[1] A policy tool which gives the government the right to use a patented product and/ or allows a third party to produce a patented product without the consent of the patentholder.
[2] A policy tool that allows the importation of a patented product marketed abroad without the consent of the patentholder.
[3] Diseases that can affect both LMICs and HICs, albeit disproportionally. Examples include HIV/AIDS and tuberculosis.
[4] Diseases that affect mostly LMICs, also called Neglected Tropical Diseases (NTDs).

diagnostics, therapeutics and vaccines. Over the past three decades, the A2M movement has worked with national governments, international health institutions and generic companies to significantly reduce the price of medicines for specific diseases in LMICs, thereby improving access to medicines and, as a result, health (for more information, see Baker, 2020).

The first phase of the A2M movement was characterised by a general homogeneity of objectives and a strategic convergence among its various constituent actors. Grassroots social movements such as the Treatment Action Campaign (TAC) in South Africa and the AIDS Coalition to Unleash Power (ACT UP) in the United States[5] led their own campaigns to raise awareness, influence health policy and the pharmaceutical research agenda, speed up clinical trials and expand access to life-saving treatments and therapies within and across countries.

A2M's strategy at the time was twofold. On the one hand, it targeted national authorities, pushing for health and social policies for people living with (and dying of) HIV and AIDS. Examples include the campaigns against South African President Thabo Mbeki and US Presidents Ronald Reagan and George H. W. Bush, whom A2M attacked for their inaction in the face of the pandemic and/or denial of its existence. In 2001, TAC also sued the South African Minister of Health for restricting access to drugs that would reduce Mother-To-Child Transmission (MTCT) of HIV (Heywood, 2003). A year later, the Constitutional Court ruled in favour of TAC and ordered the government to remove the restrictions on the availability of the treatment and to implement a comprehensive programme to prevent HIV MTCT.

In addition to strategies oriented towards national authorities, A2M also targeted the pharmaceutical industry, with campaigns such as TAC's 'Patent Rights vs. Patients' Rights' and ACT-UP's innovative boycotts and naming and shaming of pharmaceutical companies through zaps, a set of direct-action tactics that combined advocacy with public and often theatrical ridicule of those in power. The campaigns also relied on publicising drug prices and exposing the close relationship between pharmaceutical companies and the state (Gamson, 1989; Graf, 1992; Heywood, 2001; Loff & Heywood, 2002).

The South African TAC also used litigation tactics to oppose pharmaceutical conglomerates and secure access to medicines for HIV/AIDS patients. More specifically, in an ironic twist, TAC turned the legal action initiated by the Pharmaceutical Manufacturers' Association to liberalise drug pricing to its

---

[5] ACT-UP was founded in the United States, but national branches forming international collaborations were also established in Canada, the U.K. and France.

advantage, by revising the Medicines and Related Substances Control Act. As Heywood (2001: 148) notes,

> [e]ven if the Act had not been designed specifically with the AIDS epidemic in mind (which it was not: its aim was to make all drugs more affordable), the epidemic created the urgency and justification for legislative action to make drugs more affordable.

In addition to this, the movement's organisations formed broader networks based on strong international cooperation to fight the HIV/AIDS epidemic and its impact in LMICs. One example is the US-based ACT UP, which used advocacy strategies to support South Africa and expose the pro-pharma agenda of Al Gore. According to Sell (2003: 152), '[g]roup members repeatedly disrupted Vice President Al Gore's campaign appearances in the summer of 1999 with noisemakers and banners reading "Gore's Greed Kills"' (ibid.). These collective actions proved successful, and led to US President Bill Clinton announcing that the United States would

> conduct its health and trade policies in a way that ensures that people in the poorest countries don't go without the medicines they so desperately need. (quoted by Médecins Sans Frontières Access Campaign, 1999)

However, the efforts of campaigners to persuade the US government to extend this approach to all LMICs, at least as far as the HIV/AIDS crisis was concerned, ultimately failed.

The creation of international collaborations also contributed to the launch of international initiatives, including the Health GAP (Global Access Project), which was founded in the late 1990s by a network of movements and CSOs, including TAC and *Médecins Sans Frontières* (MSF) (Cassier, 2014). In addition to these struggles and campaigns, A2M also worked at the international level to adopt the Declaration on the TRIPS Agreement and Public Health at the WTO. Prior to the 2001 WTO Ministerial in Doha, the Pharmaceutical Research and Manufacturers of America presented reports arguing that problems of access to medicines were not due to the existing patent system, but rather to the poverty of LMICs and their health systems. In an organised response, the African Group at the WTO, together with Brazil and India, sought to reverse these claims and instead secure a declaration affirming the validity of TRIPS flexibilities and their use by countries without fear of retaliation. The pharmaceutical lobby, together with the US and Swiss governments, quickly joined forces to deflect the issue away from intellectual property rights. Moreover, the United States went a step further by attempting to break the solidarity among the applicant countries, offering different deals to African states- a move denounced by A2M as divisive.

The emergence of these tensions reflected the contentious nature of pharmaceutical patents, which led then WTO Director-General, Mike Moore, to identify the issue as a 'deal breaker' for the upcoming conference ('t Hoen, 2002: 42). The conflict was to be exacerbated by the 'anthrax scare' in the United States following the attacks on the Twin Towers on 11 September 2001, when Canada and the United States attempted to issue Compulsory Licences for the production of anthrax therapeutics. Although the case did not proceed, the proponents of the Doha Declaration used it as an opportunity to demonstrate the validity of their claims, and the Doha Declaration was adopted at the WTO conference later that year (for more, see Sell, 2003; 't Hoen, 2002).

The Doha Declaration emphasised the sovereignty of countries in using the existing flexibilities of the TRIPS Agreement – mainly through the policy instruments introduced earlier – and went on to elaborate on them. The Declaration of Commitment on HIV/AIDS: Global Crisis – Global Action stated that the TRIPS Agreement 'does not and should not prevent [WTO] Members from taking measures to protect public health'. Moreover, it reaffirmed

> the right of WTO members to make full use of the provisions . . . which can and should be interpreted and implemented in a manner that supports the right of WTO members to protect public health and, in particular, to promote access to medicines for all. (cited in Garattini, 2016: 357)

The Doha Declaration was the first instance in which access to medicines was publicly framed as an issue, providing the symbolic legitimacy for subsequent waves of A2M activism. However, as governments remained reluctant to use TRIPS flexibilities, the tools of Compulsory Licensing and Parallel Importation were instead used as threats by civil society actors targeting pharmaceutical companies.

Summarising this first period of A2M activism, Baker (2020) describes it as one

> of trade threats and WTO actions, Big Pharma lawsuits against progressive government action, and counter-actions by developing countries and activists in courts, at the WTO and in public arenas. (ibid.: 3)

TRIPS Plus and the Strengthening of Patents

Looking back at the developments that took place in Doha, one is left to ponder whether it was a victory for A2M or a mere reaffirmation of the original TRIPS agreement. However, following the Doha Declaration, the pharmaceutical industry and its home countries joined forces to strengthen IP protection for health-related technologies and products beyond the provisions originally agreed in TRIPS.

These provisions, informally known as TRIPS-Plus, formed part of bilateral and regional Free Trade Agreements (FTAs) and were used by the United States and Europe to mitigate the 'protection gaps' in the original TRIPS. These extensions were achieved through 'forum shifting', that is, the transfer of negotiations from the WTO and its Doha Declaration to regional and national fora, giving patent proponents more opportunities and room for manoeuvre (Lopert & Gleeson, 2013: 201). In response, and as we will see next, A2M also shifted fora and diversified its strategies to expand access to medicines.

TRIPS-Plus undoubtedly sparked a plethora of academic and policy debates about the health impacts of FTAs, particularly for LMICs. Early analyses of these agreements particularly focused on their impact on access to medicines, identifying a number of new mechanisms that could create obstacles to this goal. Indeed, TRIPS-Plus affected access to medicines by (1) extending the term of a patent, (2) introducing 'use' patents and (3) the 'linkage' mechanism, (4) strengthening data exclusivity, and (5) limiting the policy tools available to governments to challenge the patent regime established by TRIPS (Lopert & Gleeson, 2013, Abbott, 2011; Roffe & Spennemann, 2006).

In short, 'use' patents are part of the broader 'evergreening' practices that aim to extend the duration and scope of IP protection. Evergreening – that is, the patenting of minor modifications to existing medicines, as well as their uses, dosages and means of administration – is used to extend the patent holder's monopoly over an individual medicine while delaying the entry of generic alternatives into the market, thus ensuring higher prices for a longer period of time. In this sense, TRIPS-Plus has further increased the advantage held by the pharmaceutical industry and multiplied its strategic options. As one generic company told the European Commission's Director-General for Competition,

> [t]he whole point of the patenting strategy of many originator companies is to remove legal certainty. The strategy is to file as many patents as possible on all areas of the drug and create a 'minefield' for the generic to navigate. All generics know that very few patents in this larger group will be valid and infringed by the product they intend to make, but it is impossible to be certain before launch that your product will not infringe and that you will not be subject to an injunction. (quoted in Pharmaceutical Sector Inquiry Report, European Commission Director-General for Competition, 2009)

This is related to the mechanism of linkage, which refers to the formalisation of the conditionality of generic applications on the patent status of the originator product. In this sense, the (generic) applicant has to certify and notify the authorities that its product does not infringe the originator's IP. According to Son and colleagues (2018: 2),

> [n]ot surprisingly, patent linkage has been shown to have a negative impact on access to medicines by delaying generic entry and allowing the high prices of originator drugs to remain unchecked by generic competition.

Furthermore, the linkage as dictated by FTAs is stricter and more rigid than in its application in the United States and the EU, which once again is not surprising (Correa, 2006; Lopert & Gleeson, 2013). An example of such restrictive agreements and their impact on prices and access to medicines is the US-Jordan FTA, signed in 2000. According to a 2007 report by Oxfam International (2007), drug prices had increased by 20 per cent since the signing of the agreement and had begun to strain national health budgets. In addition, the FTA delayed the availability of generic alternatives for 79 per cent of new drugs introduced by twenty-one multinational pharmaceutical companies between 2002 and 2006, which could otherwise have been offered at a lower cost in generic form. Oxfam International links these delays to the consolidation of data exclusivity, which is

> a TRIPS-plus provision that creates a new system of monopoly power, separate from patents, by blocking the registration and marketing approval of generic medicines for five or more years, even when no patent exists. (Malpani, 2007 for Oxfam International)

Data exclusivity also helps to expand opportunities to increase the profit on products and delay competition from generic alternatives, as it is a tool 'designed to require generic manufacturers to generate their own clinical trial data rather than rely on the safety and efficacy findings of the branded drugs in the generic approval process' (Sell, 2007: 60).

Finally, as mentioned earlier, these bilateral and regional agreements came with 'obligations on the parties that [would] effectively preclude the exercise of flexibilities' (Abbott, 2011: 4). Indeed, TRIPS-Plus explicitly violated the Doha Declaration, as parties could delay generic competition and/or limit Compulsory Licences to emergency situations or to specific diseases for certain countries (Sell, 2007: 62–63).

FTAs and their impact on the patent system have stirred the pharmaceutical arena and exacerbated tensions within it (ibid; Baker, 2020). With access to medicines already framed as an issue, the pharmaceutical industry went to great lengths during the Doha negotiations to reframe the problem as one of 'poverty, not patents' (Sell, 2007: 47). They warned against those 'free riders' who failed to 'reward innovation' while 'devaluing patents' more broadly.

Finally, they condemned those who opposed patents as creating barriers to the development of the next 'wonder drug' (Lopert & Gleeson, 2013: 211). In this coordinated effort to delegitimise patent challengers, the pharmaceutical sector and its lobbies departed once and for all from the original compromise quoted earlier and instead sought to maximise their returns regardless of the costs associated with patented innovation.

In the face of these developments, A2M devised new strategies to combat the ever-tightening 'lockjaw of TRIPS compliance' (Baker, 2020: 24) and to circumvent the policy innovations introduced by TRIPS-Plus. According to Sell (2007: 47), during this period A2M 'advocated compulsory licensing, generic competition, parallel importation and fixed compensation rates for pharmaceutical companies'. In addition, while access remained at the heart of the mobilisation, fears about the impact of patents on innovation became more apparent and concrete. Scientists agreed with A2M activists that

> [w]hile patents can provide incentives to innovate if there is sufficient market prospect, granting too many intellectual property rights can hinder rather than accelerate innovation by creating a 'tragedy of the anticommons'. At the same time, the high prices of medicines resulting from the current innovation system continue to create barriers to access and raise serious ethical concerns. ('t Hoen et al., 2011)

More specifically, A2M combined defensive and offensive strategies of patent opposition during this period. The latter consisted mainly of the extension of waiver periods, opposition proceedings against specific patents, patent law amendments and the Medicines Patent Pool (MPP).

Patent law changes were prompted by the deadlines faced by LMICs in the mid-2000s to comply with TRIPS (minimum) standards. During this period, A2M mobilised to influence policymaking by incorporating TRIPS flexibilities into the new legal frameworks for patents. This proved to be a successful strategy in a number of LMICs, including India, which was particularly important because of its historical role as the 'pharmacy of the developing world' (Baker, 2020: 8).

The early 2000s saw the development of the Affordable Medicines and Treatment Campaign, which involved legal experts and mobilised civil society. This campaign aimed to safeguard Indian patent law by prohibiting TRIPS-Plus inspired practices, promoting government use licences and ensuring a 'very broad compulsory licensing provision' (Kapczynski, 2009: 1610). It also sought to involve civil society and the government in monitoring the impact of TRIPS on access to medicines. The campaign combined legal instruments with massive street protests, which were particularly aimed at pharmaceutical companies holding patents on antiretroviral therapies.

These successes on the Indian side not only helped boost production of generic medicines, which would benefit a number of LMICs, but they also set an example of successful mobilisation that could be replicated in other national contexts. This was important because international mobilisation and cooperation were crucial. According to the Lawyers Collective, this was due to the fact that

> [i]n each of our countries, we face various constraints in our efforts to improve access to medicines, including resource and capacity constraints (in George et al., 2009: 110).

These campaigns, orchestrated by A2M's national and international branches, increased the pressure on the pharmaceutical industry and pushed some companies to grant Voluntary Licences (VLs) to some LMICs. At the same time, A2M raised concerns about the time-consuming legal procedures for issuing VLs, which were further slowed down by the country-by-country and drug-by-drug protocol.

In response to these concerns, the movement developed a new strategy aimed at using VLs to seek global cooperation to overcome the aforementioned constraints. The Medicines Patent Pool (MPP), an independent organisation established by Unitaid in 2010, focused on LMICs with the aim of expanding access to medicines through the acquisition of VLs from patent holders and the subsequent production of generic alternatives (for more information, see 't Hoen et al., 2011). From this perspective, the MPP expanded the production and distribution of generic medicines and influenced innovation in the development of generic products. However, this triggered intra-coalitional conflicts within A2M, with criticisms coming mainly from activists focused on countries that were not (yet) part of the pool and from those who favoured more disruptive strategies. Dissatisfaction with the MPP tended to focus on VLs, which were accused of hindering more radical goals, such as IP reform and CLs. VL strategies were therefore framed as 'industry controlled', and it was argued that they were aimed at 'controlling competition' by dividing markets (Baker, 2018: 308). Segments of A2M saw these strategies as giving pharmaceutical companies excessive control over the territories covered and key licensing terms, and expressed concern that MPP and VLs strategies were better funded than opposition efforts (Baker, 2020).Conversely, proponents of VLs saw them as complementary to other access to medicines strategies, highlighting the benefits of MPP in accelerating access by bypassing the uncertainties of country-by-country opposition and CLs (Baker, 2018).

Over time, VLs have become a primary tool of patent opposition. This is not to say that opposition strategies were not pursued, particularly in response to the restriction of TRIPS flexibilities on the part of industry. Perhaps the most important such victory during this period was India's rejection of the Novartis cancer drug Glivec, which provoked a strong reaction from the company. After a series of lawsuits, the Indian Supreme Court upheld a broad interpretation of the country's amended Patent Act of 2005, stating that the drug 'did not demonstrate enhanced efficacy' and was therefore 'not patentable' (Gabble & Kohler, 2014).

In this climate of general disagreement over strategic choices and only partial victories, the United States, along with the EU, sought to further promote IP protection by drafting the Anti-Counterfeiting Trade Agreement (ACTA). ACTA became the focus of national, transnational and international controversy, bringing together a range of criticisms relating to democratic accountability, public health, innovation and freedom of expression. Although it was negotiated and signed at the WTO in 2010, its implementation was halted by popular, and ultimately political, opposition. ACTA thus presented both threats and opportunities for A2M activism during this period.

By and large, ACTA was defeated due to growing discontent in Europe and the support it was able to garner in the European Parliament. In particular, social movement analysts have explained the divergence of positions between the supportive European Commission (EC) and the hostile European Parliament (EP) as a result of national and transnational protests and their influence among Members of the European Parliament (Crespy & Parks, 2017: 12). The analysis of EU institutions and dynamics for A2M is relevant to this Element, and will be further elaborated in the following empirical section. However, as noted by Rone (2021), while the opposition to ACTA has been successful, it has mostly focused on issues of internet freedoms. As such, the European branch of A2M was the passive recipient of a campaign heralded by other actors, thus failing to take advantage of a historic opportunity to mobilise against patents on health-related products.

Bio-financialisation through the Assetisation of Patents

The third phase of A2M activism is characterised by the rapid financialisation of the pharmaceutical industry and the associated assetisation of patents. According to Birch and Muniesa (2020: 14), biopharmaceutical assetisation refers to the transformation of scientific knowledge and legal practices into 'identifiable and alienable property' that 'can be owned ... and capitalised as a source of income'. Bio-financialisation undoubtedly represents a departure from the previous period, as

[w]hereas the 'innovation' model of pharmaceutical capitalism derives its power from monopolistic control of market access through the patent regime, in the modern financialised model additional power is derived from the control of patents both as legal claims and as material manifestations of a future revenue stream. (Bourgeron & Geiger, 2022: 26)

The capitalisation of patents in recent years has certainly contributed to the steep rise in drug prices, making them unaffordable even for HICs. Perhaps the most symbolic of such protest cases was the campaign for access to sofosbuvir, an antiviral drug for hepatitis C. When first introduced, twelve weeks of sofosbuvir therapy cost an average of US$42,017: a price that health policy experts considered unsustainable even for the wealthiest health systems (Iyengar et al., 2016). According to Bourgeron and Geiger (2022), the originator company, Gilead, took the following steps to protect the intellectual property rights of sofosbuvir: (1) it converted molecules into patents, (2) it built exclusivity on a patent architecture and, finally (3), it defended the patent monopoly against civil society.

As such, the third period of A2M began in 2015, when activists from HICs and LMICs came together to contest Gilead's strategy and the impact that this price would have on health systems. The challenges to the cost of sofosbuvir marked a renewed involvement of HICs in patent opposition, building on previous experiences of HIV/AIDS activism (ibid; Chabrol et al., 2017). In addition, A2M strategically partnered with generic medicine companies to expose the 'blatant assetisation' and strengthening of scientifically weak patents. Although the movement failed to influence the rejection of the aforementioned patents, it succeeded in discursively challenging Gilead's patent strategy.

The struggles over sofosbuvir led to the formation of two transnational alliances: the Benelux Initiative and the Valletta Declaration. Both networks involve HICs from the European continent, with the stated aim of sharing pricing information and pursuing collective negotiations with pharmaceutical companies (Natsis, 2017; Stafford, 2017). What is more, the collaboration between HICs and LMICs during the 2019 World Health Assembly led to the development of the Transparency Resolution, which calls on member states to improve transparency on pharmaceutical pricing, negotiations and clinical trial results (Bourgeron & Geiger, 2022).

Beyond the issue of pricing, and building on the sofosbuvir case, over this period A2M insisted on attacking patents in the name of innovation. Since the development of the modern patent regime under TRIPS, pharmaceutical companies have defended IP and their drug prices as necessary for the R&D of new therapeutics and diagnostics. In response to this rationalisation and justification of the IP regime, activists have suggested that rather than advancing knowledge and innovation in socially valuable directions, the current system of incentives redirects R&D towards profitable paths that stagnate knowledge (see also Cameron & Berger, 2005; Gøtzsche, 2018; Sellin, 2015).

During this period, especially in HICs, A2M has devoted time and resources in developing and publicising alternative systems of medical innovation, exploring different incentives for R&D and portraying the current patent system economically and scientifically unsustainable. An example of this strategy – which is intended to develop in parallel with the patent challenge – can be found in A2M's delinkage campaign, which aims to transform the funding of health-related R&D, while (gradually) removing the dependence of R&D funding on high prices. It aims to establish global norms for R&D funding that go beyond the current IP system. This would be done through global agreements on R&D funding, cross-border cooperation and agreements on public goods. Progressive delinkage suggests that this transition from one system of R&D to another should be achieved through a combination of voluntary and mandatory approaches to address both short-term objectives and long-term policy goals.[6]

This on delinkage in HICs has provoked further disagreement within the broader health movement. Activists in LMICs, in particular, saw this strategic focus on R&D and the sustainability of the patent regime as a move away from access issues per se. They insisted that A2M should focus on patent challenges and use TRIPS flexibilities to address the most pressing barriers to access. Activists in HICs, on the other hand, argued that problems of access for all should be addressed at the root of the problem, by creating alternative systems of innovation.

These tensions were further fuelled by developments in the political economy of the largest pharmaceutical companies. In the words of Baker (2020: 32),

> [a]dvocates of domestic drug pricing argue that reform of global IP structures and trade policies cannot occur unless people in rich countries, whose governments support IP maximisation, realise the harm that IP maximisation does to their own health. They argue that access to the latest breakthrough therapies is being rationed even in the US and Europe, where an affordability crisis threatens government, institutional and individual payers. If excessive pricing reform is achieved through intellectual property flexibilities, price controls, competition policy and other reforms in rich countries, they hope that citizens in these countries might eventually express more solidarity with people living with inadequate access to affordable medicines in LMICs.

---

[6] https://delinkage.org/mechanics/.

During this period of increasing pressure, A2M expanded its activism beyond HIV/AIDS drugs and treatments to other types of diseases – including the aforementioned hepatitis C – and mobilised activists in HICs to defend their own health systems from the aggressive pricing strategies of the pharmaceutical industry. Baker (2020) identifies a dual movement of expansion and contraction for A2M. Specifically, the movement opened up to new medicines and treatments, appealing to new constituencies – patient groups – that were crucial for mobilising A2M activism. In addition, A2M increasingly directed its activism towards international fora, seeking legitimacy from the WHO and the UN, while also targeting the national level for greater transparency and regulation. At the same time, however, the increased pressures resulting from the biofinancialisation of the industry led to an inward turn among HIC activists, who began to prioritise issues of transparency, innovation and the sustainability of the patent regime over issues of access in LMICs.

Conclusion

In this section we have seen the reciprocal influences of the modern patent regime and A2M activism. What we have recounted is a story of the biopolitical capture of public goods with serious implications for the right to health evoked in the first section of this Element. In addition to a brief history of patents and their discontents, we have looked at how political opportunities have affected action repertoires, organisational models and collective frames, and have divided the movement. Finally, we have attempted to shed light on the international, transnational and national political economy of health-related innovations and products, providing some relevant information on the context in which the announcement of Covid-19 as a pandemic took place.

3 The 'No Profit on Pandemic' Initiative in the EU

In Europe, as in other regions, the pandemic prompted discussions about public health and healthcare, highlighting the need for a closer examination of the interconnections and underlying factors of these two fields. At a joint press conference with the WHO in April 2020, EC President Ursula von der Leyen announced that

> [w]e need to develop a vaccine. We need to produce it and to deploy it to every single corner of the world. And make it available at affordable prices. This vaccine will be our universal, common good. (European Commission, 2020)

The statement concluded with a pledge of international solidarity, affirming that

> [t]he European Union will spare no effort to help the world come together against coronavirus. Because united we will make history with a global response to the global pandemic. (ibid.)

Subsequently, the A2M network in Europe initiated the 'No Profit On Pandemic.EU' European Citizens' Initiative (ECI) in July 2020, with the objective of proposing legislative action to the EC to guarantee global access to medicines for the treatment of Covid-19.

In the preceding section, the evolution of the patent regime and its discontents were examined. It was observed that the TRIPS Agreement, which was concluded during the HIV/AIDS pandemic, encountered resistance through the formation of a transnational network of activists, national governments and generic drug manufacturers who mobilised against the patent system and in defence of public health. As will be demonstrated in this and the following section, the advent of the Covid-19 pandemic presented both opportunities and challenges for the mobilisation of A2M. At the European Union level, the 'No Profit on Pandemic' campaign built upon existing achievements, while also reflecting the internal divisions within the movement for health rights. In particular, we will demonstrate the challenges encountered by the campaign in surmounting the formidable lobbying efforts of the pharmaceutical industry and in influencing the centralised and opaque decision-making process at the EU level. Furthermore, we identify and examine the internal tensions within the movement. We contend that the cumulative impact of these challenges has resulted in the inability to achieve universal and equitable access to a Covid-19 vaccine in Europe. This shortcoming has global ramifications. Concurrently, we will illustrate how the campaign prompted collective and individual contemplation on the movement's tactics, organisational models and collective framing, which are essential for further mobilisation on the issue of health rights.

The following section presents the campaign for the ECI within the context of the EU institutions. This is followed by an analysis of the data collected regarding three key areas: the campaign's action repertoires, organisational networks and collective frames. In doing so, we will examine the opportunities and challenges faced by the European branch of A2M during the pandemic.

The 'No Profit on Pandemic' European Citizens' Initiative in Context

The pandemic precipitated an unparalleled degree of EU involvement in health matters, culminating in the reinforcement of the historically underdeveloped and peripheral European health policy (Brooks et al., 2023; Greer et al., 2021). This historic weakness has been attributed to the EU's primary development as a market entity, with responsibility for the implementation of redistributive policies, including healthcare, being devolved to the Member States (Greer & Jarman, 2021). However, the pandemic presented a challenge to this status quo. Despite not formally reducing the health competencies of Member States, the EU assumed an active role in coordinating national efforts and facilitating cooperation to end the pandemic. The EU's pandemic response has been perceived as a pivotal moment, characterised by expeditious action in the name of internal solidarity, in stark contrast to the management of the financial crisis. Examples of this shift include the suspension of the Stability and Growth Pact and the creation of NextGenerationEU and the Resilience and Recovery Facility (Boin & Rhinard, 2023; della Porta et al., 2022; Quaglia & Verdun, 2023). These initiatives allocated funds towards the strengthening of healthcare systems in the short- and medium-term, although their orientation and impact remain to be examined (Galanti & Christou, forthcoming).

Moreover, notable developments were observed in the field of transnational health policy, with proposals for the establishment of a 'European Health Union' in response to the challenges posed by the pandemic (Guy, 2023; McKee & Ruijter, 2024). The Commission would be responsible for the establishment of the Union, which would entail assuming responsibility for central purchasing and redistribution, as well as for the setting up and management of the RescEU emergency stockpile and the EU4Health long-term stockpile initiative, with a view to ensuring redistribution at the European level. As Greer et al. (2021: 46) observe, this represented a 'considerable step forward', given that these initiatives address a significant gap in the current regimes, which are voluntary and intergovernmental. Moreover, the Commission reinterpreted the concept of public health derogation from the national level to a concept of European public health and solidarity regarding freedom of movement (de Ruijter et al., 2020).

It is notable that the pandemic served to advance the role of the EC and its President in the procurement and distribution of vaccines within Europe and beyond. In June 2020, the EC and the Ministers of Health from the Member States reached an agreement on a joint approach to vaccine procurement, whereby the Commission was tasked with negotiating, purchasing and allocating vaccines. The unprecedented Europeanisation of health policy and the enhanced role of the Commission, particularly in relation to vaccines, initiated a transnational approach and influenced the orientation of anti-patent contention during this emergency critical juncture.

This orientation of contention was further reinforced after the Commission's decision to disengage from its global commitments. While acknowledging the transnationalisation of health and vaccine policy spearheaded by the European Commission during the pandemic, scholars also highlight its regionalisation. As Deters and Zardo (2023) observe, following the EC's assertion of leadership in the transnational and international responses to the pandemic, President von der Leyen called for global action and solidarity and, in collaboration with the WHO, established the COVAX initiative, which was a key component of the multilateral response to the pandemic. However, once the EC assumed a leadership role in global health governance, solidarity faltered and global collaboration progressed more slowly (Deters and Zardo, 2023: 1051).

By June 2020, the EC had devised a strategy for the distribution of the Covid-19 vaccine based on three key objectives: (1) ensuring the quality, safety, and efficacy of vaccines; (2) securing timely access to vaccines for member states and their populations, while leading a global solidarity effort; and (3) ensuring equitable access for all to an affordable vaccine as early as possible. The strategy was based on the production and procurement of sufficient vaccine doses for each member state through Advance Purchase Agreements (APAs) negotiated with vaccine producers (Sciacchitano & Bartolazzi, 2021).

These developments collectively resulted in the registration of the 'No Profit On Pandemic.EU' European Citizens' Initiative (ECI) with the European Commission in July 2020. The ECI is an instrument that was established by the Treaty of Lisbon in 2009 with the objective of enabling European citizens to submit legislative proposals to the European Commission. Presented as a means of enhancing access to the EU level and fostering citizen involvement, the ECI process has undergone modifications over time, with the objective of streamlining and accelerating the procedure (European Parliament, 2023).

In general, the criteria for a successful ECI are quite stringent, and the potential for it to serve as a vehicle for empowering citizens is relatively limited. In order to propose legislative action to the EC it is necessary to collect signatures from one million EU citizens, which must be gathered from at least one quarter of the Member States, each meeting specific minimum thresholds. Should the campaign succeed in amassing the requisite signatures, the Commission is obliged to reach a decision on the proposal within a period of three months. This entails conducting a meeting with the campaigners and a public hearing at the European Parliament. Notwithstanding the amendments that have been made to the instrument, it remains a challenging tool for mobilisation as it necessitates both effective organisation and civic participation at the transnational level. As of

March 2021, of the 78 initiatives that have been registered since the establishment of the ECI tool, only five were successful in collecting the required number of signatures, and none have yet resulted in direct policy changes (Drugau-Constantin & Anghel-Sienerth, 2022).

Consequently, the ECI has become the subject of academic and political scrutiny due to its rigidity and limited effectiveness in relation to civil society. A review of the literature reveals a number of reasons for the failure of the majority of ECIs to collect the required number of signatures, as well as the overall weakness of the instrument in achieving more than just a discussion at the Commission level (della Porta & Parks, 2018; Drugau-Constantin & Anghel-Sienerth, 2022; Szabó et al., 2022; Weisskircher, 2020). Furthermore, the ECI has been criticised for being ill-suited to transnational campaigns, as its structure tends to prioritise the promotion of national campaigns in larger Member States. Finally, involvement in ECIs frequently results in disappointment with the instrument, often prompting activists to revert to national-level organisation and mobilisation (Weisskircher, 2020).

Once registered, the 'No Profit on Pandemic' ECI was required to collect one million signatures across Europe within one year (with an additional six months granted due to the health emergency) in order for it to be considered by the Commission. The campaign, which adopted the label 'Right to Cure' (a designation previously used by several unsuccessful initiatives before the pandemic), sought to 'propose concrete legislative action to the European Commission' (European Citizens' Initiative, n.d.). As will be demonstrated, the campaign for the ECI mobilised the traditional repertoire of action of A2M, with only limited innovations to adapt to the health emergency and to expand the mobilised networks behind A2M in this juncture. Ultimately, the frames developed and advocated by A2M during this period were firmly embedded in the historical traditions of the movement, while also reflecting its internal divisions. This ultimately proved ineffective in fostering greater convergence between the Global North and the Global South.

The Repertoire of Action: Sensitisation without Protest?

As previously stated, the primary strategy of the European branch of A2M during the pandemic was to concentrate its efforts on an ECI targeting the EC. In spite of the fact that it was not a particularly popular choice, this tool was selected as the principal vehicle for contention during the pandemic, given the limitations of other types of protest due to the state of emergency and the centrality of the EC in managing the health crisis (Christou & della Porta, 2024).

In general, progressive social movements reacted to the pandemic by adapting to the constraints on the rights of movement and assembly imposed during the health emergency. This involved the use of blended, distanced and symbolic forms of action (della Porta, 2022: 28). As previously stated, like numerous other transnational campaigns, A2M has historically favoured moderate, insider-oriented forms of contention, which have at times been complemented by more disruptive tactics, including marches, zaps, die-ins and direct action. In the context of the global pandemic caused by Covid-19, members of the A2M movement opted to invest in an ECI with the dual objective of influencing decision-making at the EC level through the petition itself, while also advancing their advocacy agenda through the campaign effort.

The decision to pursue an ECI was consistent with the traditional repertoire of contention employed by the A2M movement. Despite being a relatively novel tactic within the context of the A2M, the choice of the ECI was shaped by the Europeanisation of health policy during the pandemic and the central role assumed by the EC in this process. Furthermore, the ascendance of the Commission to a pivotal position in the negotiations, coupled with its role in procuring and distributing vaccines across Europe and beyond, provided a rationale for the A2M's strategic focus on the Commission throughout this period, which was facilitated by the ECI.

In a recent interview, Julie Steendam, the ECI campaign coordinator for the People's Health Movement (PHM), highlighted the unique challenges associated with engaging with the EU and the European Commission. As she notes, the choice to launch the ECI also built upon an existing organisational network of previous campaigns, even if it was broadened over the pandemic through a tried and tested, routinised process:

> the starting point [was] to build a network, because of course you need a lot of organisations at different levels in all the countries to collect this number of signatures ... We started with the network that we had- actually with the PHM. So thanks to previous campaign work, previous networking work of the People's Health Movement, we were already in contact with quite some groups of people, or organisations all over Europe. So this was amazing. We extended the network by also, for example, contacting better-known groups, NGOs like Oxfam, Greenpeace, Amnesty International. They're quite used to launching these European Citizens' Initiatives ... So in the end, we had a network or a list of about 360 supporting organisations, which is a huge number and it's quite impressive ... [In addition] we used the contacts of

political parties ... We got a lot of advice and support from the Left in the European Parliament. (interview no. 3)

In light of the restrictions imposed on physical movement and mobilisation in public spaces as a result of the pandemic, the campaign was primarily conducted online, as was the case for numerous other initiatives at the time, and was brokered by prominent NGOs. Furthermore, the skills acquired in digital activism by NGOs, coupled with their capacity to attract influential media personalities, served to enhance the aforementioned brokerage. As our interlocutors observed, the number of signatures garnered in response to a single influencer video posted on the website or Instagram page of a large NGO would far surpass the results achieved through traditional canvassing tactics. Over time, this had the effect of further discouraging grassroots organisation and mobilisation.

The format of the online petition, however, presented significant challenges for the organisers. Firstly, the fact that online petitions for the ECI do not disclose signatory information to the organisers makes it challenging for them to maintain campaign momentum, expand their organisational networks and/or fund their activities. This had implications for the likelihood of success for the initiative, as well as the development and consolidation of anti-patent contestation. In order to achieve their objective, Julie Steendam explained that it was necessary to implement a two-step strategy for signing the document. Consequently, the collection of signatures served to facilitate the involvement of individuals, maintain communication and potentially solicit donations for the campaign. However, with 'each [and] every step you add to the process of signing the ECI you risk losing signatures' (Interview no. 3).

Furthermore, the specific limitations on forms of contention during the pandemic significantly impacted the tactics selected to advance the campaign for the ECI. In particular, several interviewees discussed the necessity of adapting their strategies to align with the varying national regulations on social distancing in order to facilitate the promotion of protests. One interviewee highlighted the challenges encountered when PHM Europe sought to organise a European Day of Action across different national contexts. She told us that

> [PHM] wanted to have small scale, safely organised actions in squares and streets on the same day. In Belgium, this was happening all the time. So [it was] easy to organise. Italy too – not an issue. Spain completely okay. But then in Ireland it was a no-go. It was still taboo to organise something outside because it would really ... take away all the authority of your health group. (ibid.)

In response to this challenge, campaigners explored digital alternatives to traditional campaigning tactics, particularly if they sought to engage with transnational audiences.

Moreover, the well-structured organisations within the campaign had an advantage over grassroots social movement actors, due to the digital skills shared by employees as well as their more extensive experience in dealing with petitions. This resulted in the former brokering the campaign, which, in turn, led to the actions of the movement being constrained.

Additionally, the campaign sought to influence European politics by engaging with members of the national and European parliaments. National branches, such as that of Italy, were particularly efficacious in advancing their agenda to national parliamentarians, while the organisers of the ECI were successful in garnering the support of the European Left in the EP.

In conclusion, the A2M campaign in Europe did not demonstrate notable tactical innovation over the course of the period under review. Instead, it adapted its advocacy and campaigning activities to align with the health measures imposed by the pandemic.

Organisational Network: Loosened and Cleaved?

As previously stated, A2M is a loosely structured network of collective actors. The social movements that form part of this network are also loosely organised, comprising a variety of actors, including grassroots trade unions, patients' groups, environmental and peace activists, among others. The expansion of the constituencies of A2M over the period was facilitated by the proliferation of health rights, which enabled a greater number of diverse actors to engage in discussions about public health and care. These discussions were characterised by expressions of anxiety and criticism concerning the role of the pharmaceutical industry in profiting from these issues (Christou, 2024; della Porta & Lavizzari, 2022).

The ECI campaign engaged a diverse array of organisational networks, including A2M activists, and reached out to groups concerned with access to medicines that had previously been uninvolved, including feminist, peace, alterglobalist, ecologist and human rights social movement organisations, as well as religious groups. Despite originating from disparate traditions, these groups unified in their efforts to safeguard health from commercial interests and uphold health rights. Nevertheless, the transnational organisation of the network encountered a number of challenges, which ultimately resulted in the failure of the campaign to obtain the requisite number of signatures.

Firstly, the potential for success and the pace of progress varied considerably from one national context to another. As our interlocutors posited, the ultimate success of the ECI campaign hinged on the pre-pandemic infrastructure of A2M activism. As the PHM Coordinator for Europe observed, the situation in PHM

France was particularly favourable, due to the group's high level of activity. In essence, they were able to generate momentum and forge connections with other organisations, trade unions and women's groups in France, thereby laying the groundwork for the signature collection efforts. In other locations, however, there was a lack of organisational capacity to effectively spearhead the campaign. As such, the extent of success 'kind of depend[ed] on how active people were before. And how they felt that the topic resonated with them locally' (interview no. 2).

The strength of local infrastructure prior to the pandemic was of great consequence with regard to the organisational resources and networks necessary for the advancement of the campaign. Additionally, it was of considerable importance with respect to national traditions and the comprehension of A2M. As our interlocutors observed, the countries that were able to collect the requisite number of signatures (namely, Belgium, Ireland, Italy and the Netherlands) were those with the most active A2M milieu and networks.

A second challenge identified by the organisers interviewed was the varying perceptions of the EU across the different EU countries. As indicated by the organisers, the degree of approval (or disapproval) enjoyed by the EU and its institutions within the local context exerted a considerable influence on the success of the campaign in each of the countries. The campaign was therefore more successful in contexts where the EU, and in particular the Commission, was regarded as a relevant political target, as opposed to situations where it was viewed as superfluous and/or unresponsive to the concerns of citizens.

This consideration is also linked to perceptions regarding the ECI tool. In response to our questions regarding the rationale behind the decision to utilise the ECI as the primary instrument of the European A2M campaign, our interlocutors drew attention to the fact that the ECI itself was the subject of contention, particularly among a number of prominent organisations. Indeed, our interlocutors questioned the efficacy of the ECI strategy, citing frequent advice from organisations with extensive ECI experience to pursue alternative avenues, given the perceived limitations of the ECI as a means of influencing the EC. These concerns represented significant challenges for the organisers, as hostility and scepticism towards the ECI hindered the potential for coalitions to be formed between A2M advocates and larger advocacy and contentious networks.

Furthermore, the capacity of the campaigners to cultivate transnational momentum was constrained by the varying levels of influence and strength of the pharmaceutical industry across diverse national contexts. In certain countries, such as Germany, the considerable influence and resources possessed by the pharmaceutical industry presented a significant challenge for campaigners seeking to gain traction and mobilise support. This disparity in the strength of the industry created an uneven playing field, which impeded the overall cohesion and effectiveness of the campaign at the transnational level. Furthermore, the organisers reported difficulties in garnering support from countries where the pharmaceutical industry is highly influential. Signatories were reluctant to position themselves in opposition to a significant pillar of their national economy.

The aforementioned organisational challenges were further compounded by the inherent obstacles presented by the pandemic emergency. The organisers informed us of their ongoing endeavours to innovate their forms of communication, their repeated meetings with the objective of facilitating transnational coordination, and the numerous webinars they conducted with a view to advancing their advocacy efforts. However, as the pandemic response developed rapidly and unevenly across Europe, both national and transnational networks consistently encountered delays in aligning with the latest developments.

Collective Framing: the Meaning of Health for All

The frames of the campaign are collectively defined by the overarching phrase 'Health for All', as expressed in the call for the ECI, which entailed the guarantee of extensive and expeditious global access to research and technologies, as well as the opposition to patents that impede availability and augment costs. This is one of the core frames of A2M historically, and the pandemic presented an opportune moment to advance it.

The second claim was summarised in the phrase 'Transparency Now', with calls to ensure transparency regarding production costs, public contributions and contract details. This claim can be situated within the more recent traditions of A2M, particularly in HICs, as discussed in the preceding section. As previously stated, over the period in question the negotiations and procurement of Covid-19 vaccines were delegated to the EC, with particular responsibility resting with the then-President of the EC, Ursula von der Leyen. One year after the ECI campaign commenced, members of the press and CSOs began to voice concerns about the opacity of the negotiations. As Kenneth Haar, a researcher at Corporate Europe Observatory, has observed,

> [t]he global negotiations on patents on vaccines, medicines and diagnostics is one of the most important negotiations currently taking place internationally– this is about the best way to end the pandemic. And yet, the first and only time this was addressed by the [European] Council, they keep it secret. The general public should not accept that, given the hugely negative impact the pandemic has had on their lives. In particular, members of parliaments, the European Parliament not least, should not let this secrecy and lack of transparency pass. (Corporate Europe Observatory, 2021b)

Furthermore, Kate Elder, Senior Vaccines Policy Advisor for MSF's Access Campaign, asserted that ' [t]he public has the right to know what's in these deals ... There is no place for secrets during a pandemic; there is too much at stake' (Médecins Sans Frontières Access Campaign, 2020b).

The secrecy of the negotiations was the result of the pharmaceutical industry's successful lobbying efforts, which served to enhance the opaque implications of IP. The pharmaceutical lobby is identified as a significant adversary, benefitting from preferential and unjust treatment from the Commission through the utilisation of the protections afforded by 'industry secrets'. In this context, pharmaceutical conglomerates are presented as unified in their opposition to the joint procurement mechanism for vaccines, diagnostics and therapeutics. They exploited competition between countries for medical products to address the pandemic. Once negotiations regarding vaccines commenced, the pharmaceutical industry leveraged its oligopoly power to further its influence, requesting the Commission's assistance in reducing the risks associated with purchasing and administering vaccines (Corporate Europe Observatory, 2021a; Peigne, 2021).

Furthermore, Vaccine Europe, a division of the European Federation of Pharmaceutical Industries and Associations (EFPIA), sought assurances from the Commission regarding indemnification for 'certain liabilities' arising from the 'inevitable risks' of vaccine administration (Peel & Mancini, 2020). The industry demanded that the negotiations be conducted in complete secrecy. By June 2020, Advanced Purchase Agreements (APAs) for vaccine production, purchase and supply had been concluded between the Commission and various pharmaceutical companies, in accordance with the Commission's mandate to promote Covid-19 vaccines as global public goods.

The establishment of APAs resulted from the pharmaceutical industry's effective lobbying, which primarily served to 'incentivise' and de-risk pharmaceutical investment. Examples of this include first purchase contracts, such those between CureVac and the EC, where the latter would pay two-thirds of the total price prior to the authorisation of the vaccine by the European Medicines Agency (EMA). In other instances, the Commission has been the subject of criticism for bearing the costs associated with the final 'Fill & Finish' phase of production. Furthermore, the aforementioned APAs included clauses that prohibited Member States and the EU as a whole from donating or exporting purchased vaccines, thereby impeding international solidarity in vaccine distribution. Moreover, the agreements permitted pharmaceutical companies to terminate the supply of vaccines unilaterally in the event of delays in payments from governments or the Commission. Conversely, the Commission or national governments could only suspend payments in the event of a company's failure to deliver the agreed number of doses.

However, even in such instances, a judge would first need to determine whether the company had made the 'best reasonable effort' to provide the promised doses (F_barca, 2021).

The issue of transparency was linked to the third demand put forward in the ECI, namely 'Public Money, Public Control'. Since the advent of vaccines, numerous reports have been published that have highlighted the crucial role played by the public sector in the rapid development of vaccines. Organisers that we spoke to frequently cited the importance of collaboration between private companies and public institutions in the rapid creation of vaccines during the pandemic. From the outset of the negotiations and the rollout of the initial vaccines, it became widely known that these vaccines were developed based on public and publicly accessible knowledge, supported by substantial levels of public funding.

The campaign, thus, highlighted the crucial role of public funds in the development of vaccines, citing the contributions of prominent research institutions, such as the United States National Institutes of Health (NIH) and the University of Oxford, which were instrumental in advancing the scientific understanding of vaccines and the mRNA technology that was utilised in producing an effective Covid-19 vaccine. A substantial proportion of the research and development costs were met by public funding, primarily from the United States, the United Kingdom and Germany. The campaigners frequently invoked the case of AstraZeneca, which received 97 per cent of the funding for the development of its vaccine from public sources (Cross et al., 2021; Pilling et al., 2021; Safi, 2021).

In conclusion, the aforementioned arguments collectively reinforced the ECI's call for 'No Profit on Pandemic'. Although this is a central claim of A2M over its history, the pandemic context facilitated its diffusion, as it highlighted the incompatibility of patents with public health and pointed to the real profiteering drive of the pharmaceutical industry in developing and circulating vaccines.

However, despite the efficacy of the aforementioned frames, A2M was unable to fully capitalise on the discursive opportunities presented by the pandemic. This is mostly related to the technical nature of the patent system and, consequently, the inherent complexities associated with it. In particular, our interlocutors highlighted their difficulty in popularising certain issues and demands that have become increasingly apparent to the movement over time. Furthermore, as vaccine scepticism grew during the vaccination rollout in various European countries, local organisers encountered challenges in maintaining and articulating a critique of the pharmaceutical industry without undermining the credibility of the vaccine itself. As one Italian activist observed,

> the problem of this campaign – which is not the problem of the campaign but of the context in which the campaign developed – was the enormous difficulty of being able to reach everyone in a clear and well-defined way. Again, that's not because of the campaign *per se* but precisely because of the context in which we were immersed at that moment, that is, talking about vaccines at that time, sometimes without even having the opportunity to explain [yourself] properly, you risk being confused with those who do not even want to hear about vaccines ... I am quite convinced that the whole 'anti-vax' wave really damaged our campaign [which was already] complex because it did not aim at the government but at the European level. (interview no. 9)

Moreover, in line with the history of A2M, our interlocutors indicated that the discursive opportunity and global solidarity faltered once vaccines were purchased and became widely available in Europe. As the organisers informed us, once the vaccination programmes commenced, they were compelled to modify their frames and strategies in order to appeal to the 'logical self-interest of European citizens' (interview no. 3). This entailed a shift in focus for local campaigners, from global solidarity to the urgency of resolving the global pandemic, which was increasingly threatened by the various mutations of the coronavirus. Consequently, the concept of solidarity with the Global South had to be reframed in a more pragmatic manner. As Julie Steendam told us

> I think the Covid-19 pandemic kind of gave us the hope: Okay, we will have this perfect campaign because everybody wants to have the vaccine, everybody needs the medication, the treatment, and so on. So, from the beginning it was really more like a global, concern-everyone campaign. (ibid.)

Nevertheless, once vaccines were developed and Europe began purchasing them, the dynamics and difficulties observed in earlier periods soon resurfaced. As Ana Vračar, Regional Coordinator of PHM Europe, observed, campaigners were soon confronted with perplexity on the part of Europeans who had ceased to regard patents as an impediment to ending the pandemic. In elucidating the rationale behind the shift in strategy in light of vaccine acquisition in Europe, she stated

> [a]nd so then you talk about the whole process of it, you know, about how public funding is being used, how transparent that is, then it became a bit- it was a bit easier. It was a bit easier to maybe find that 'click'. With people who maybe do not think in global terms ... in terms of Global South and Global North. (interview no. 2)

Julie Steendam further illustrates their tactical and strategic configuration against the fast-changing landscape in Europe:

> [t]he arguments and our way of bringing forward the problem of course shifted because reality was shifting. When we started the campaign, there were no vaccines. There was just this race to make the first vaccine ... I think in this timing, the frame was interesting for health campaigners because, for the first time, it was really a health-related campaign that was important for everyone ... Of course then things started to change. Each country started to purchase vaccines. It really shifted into more like the familiar North-South solidarity campaign. Like Europe had its vaccines, but the South was left behind completely. Which really limited the message that we could bring about, but also limited the audience that we could reach because not everyone is sensitive to the ethics behind this. The other argument was price, but not everyone realises that the price that we are paying is way too much ... So, we had a dual campaign; the North-South solidarity or everyone should have access campaign, but also [one about how] we have to protect our health system and health budgets. (interview no. 3)

The global solidarity aspect of the campaign was subsequently adapted to address the self-interest of Europeans, and the frame was swiftly altered to emphasise global interconnectedness, the emergence of new variants of the virus, and the risks that even those who had already received the vaccine faced. Furthermore, as evidenced in the interviews and documents collected, concerns pertaining to transparency and democratic accountability on the part of European institutions and major pharmaceutical companies also emerged more prominently in Europe as national vaccination campaigns commenced.

In this context, the arguments pertaining to transparency and profiteering lost their efficacy once vaccines were purchased within Europe. As our respondents indicated, this was based on the erroneous assumption that vaccines were inexpensive or even free, given their extensive and cost-free provision by European healthcare systems. The available evidence indicates that the prices of vaccines have varied across different vaccines and different national contexts. For example, Dyer (2021) notes that the respective companies have charged different prices for the same vaccine in different countries. The lack of information on the net costs of vaccine production leaves us with the question of whether the costs of developing and manufacturing vaccines, net of public subsidies, justify the prices charged by vaccine producers, or whether the prices are excessive (Hassan et al., 2021; see also Light & Lexchin, 2021).

Conclusion

In conclusion, the advent of the Covid-19 pandemic presented novel prospects for A2M activism. As demonstrated in this section, the pandemic presented a pivotal moment for the movement, offering the opportunity to capitalise on the heightened attention that health rights and IP issues had garnered. This momentum was driven by public opinion, mainstream media debates and institutional support from entities such as the European Committee of the Regions and the European Parliament. Given the nature of the virus, the campaign also benefitted from a global focus on access to vaccines, which highlighted the interconnectedness of health issues and the urgent need for solidarity. As such, and in line with the relevant literature, we observe the 'Europeanisation' of health governance (Christou and della Porta, 2024) and trace the transnationalisation of anti-patent contestation over this period (Boli & Thomas 1999; della Porta, Kriesi & Rucht 1999; della Porta & Tarrow 2005; Smith et al., 1994).

Following a period of organised attacks by the pharmaceutical industry and related splits among its territories, namely those pertaining to pharmaceuticals and diseases, A2M was presented with an opportunity to reunite and challenge the patent system in a manner similar to that it had employed in response to the HIV/AIDS pandemic.

However, the campaign was impacted by internal and external challenges. Firstly, issues inherent to transnational mobilisation were encountered, which faced obstacles due to strategic divergences, differing national perceptions of the EU, and the varying strength of national groups. This vulnerability was further compounded by the pronounced alignment of the pharmaceutical industry with the EC throughout the course of the pandemic. This alignment served to advance the interests of the pharmaceutical industry while simultaneously stifling criticisms. This alignment, which will be further explored in the following section, is not a new phenomenon. As 't Hoen (2002) notes, the EC Directorate-General for Trade held this position as early as 1998, during discussions and deliberations over the WHO's Revised Drug Strategy, during which he affirmed that 'no priority should be given to health over intellectual property considerations' (European Commission, 1998, cited in 't Hoen, 2002: 36).

The coordination of activities at the transnational and national levels presented an additional challenge, with variations in multilevel discursive and political opportunities. The approach adopted by A2M with regard to the European Left at the level of the EP, which has historically demonstrated a greater openness to contesting voices (Crespy & Parks, 2017), proved nonetheless inadequate for the purpose of promoting the campaign and influencing the stance of the Commission. As one of the organisers informed us, members of the campaign expressed disappointment when the European Parliament voted in favour of TRIPS flexibilities for the duration of the pandemic, only for this to be disregarded by the European Commission.

Furthermore, the campaign encountered challenges in navigating national sensitivities. Europe's role in global pharmaceutical production presented a challenge to the articulation of critiques and the formation of global solidarity. These obstacles were compounded by the difficulty in articulating popularised critiques without inadvertently feeding into anti-vaccine narratives. Additionally, the campaign was undermined by systemic global inequalities, as the seemingly easy and free distribution of vaccine doses to European citizens appeased sentiments towards the pharmaceutical industry. This is linked to the global fragmentation in claims and organisational structures within the A2M network, which originated from the previous period of A2M activism, and it is something that hindered the effectiveness of the campaign.

4 Mobilising for Universal Access to Covid-19 Vaccines: The Campaign in Support of India and South Africa's Patent Waiver Proposal

In October 2020, amidst international negotiations on vaccines and growing concerns about the impact that these negotiations may have on LMICs, India and South Africa applied to the WTO for patent waivers for Covid-19 therapeutics, vaccines and diagnostics (People's Health Movement n.d.). The two countries (both with extensive experience in patent challenges and, in the case of India, a substantial level of infrastructure for manufacturing generic medicines) requested the removal of patents and their licensing for the national production of Covid-19 technologies and products.

Their call for a waiver extended to all countries, as they asked the WTO to allow member states to choose not to grant or enforce patents on all Covid-19-related innovations until global herd immunity was achieved. International civil society organisations joined the broad networks of health justice actors in supporting a global waiver. The proposal was supported by a number of Member States and some 300 institutions and civil society organisations worldwide, including international NGOs, transnational trade unions, academics, legal activist groups and the WHO. The EU, together with Australia, Brazil, Canada, Japan, Norway, Switzerland and the United Kingdom, either did not support or opposed the proposal, effectively blocking it in the Council for Trade-Related Aspects of Intellectual Property Rights.

The United States supported it, but only for vaccines (Médecins Sans Frontières Access Campaign, 2020a).

The failure of the waiver proposal marked the beginning of a protracted international A2M campaign, which maintained momentum for longer than expected and in some ways heralded the ECI campaign. However, the failure of the campaign to influence the WTO eventually redirected A2M activists back to more familiar fora, including the WHO and its deliberations and negotiations on the 'Pandemic Prevention, Preparedness and Response Agreement', also known as the Pandemic Treaty.

In this section, we will present and analyse the opportunities and challenges facing this international campaign for A2M. After introducing the context of the campaign, we will discuss the tactical dilemmas faced by the organisers and the choices they made, the heterogeneous organisational infrastructure mobilised, their attempts to bridge frames and the tensions created by the sum of the aforementioned.

The Global Patent Waiver Campaign in Context

The Covid-19 pandemic represented a critical juncture when health movement organisations – which were already mobilised at a global level – saw the opportunity to launch a truly global campaign. While the pandemic had made inequality in access to health most visible, it had also stimulated growing attention to its reversibility points. Since the pandemic was, by definition, a global phenomenon, some international organisations assumed a central role in articulating policies to bring it to an end. However, although the WHO became more visible – despite its failed attempts to intervene meaningfully in previous pandemics – it was the role of one of the most secretive and powerful international organisations that proved to be the most decisive: the World Trade Organization. The patent regime became a major target for those fighting for free access to vaccines.

In this section, we will present and analyse the international campaign for patent waivers, focusing on the opportunities and challenges presented by the pandemic as perceived by the main campaign organisers. Building on the previous section, we will argue that the Covid-19 pandemic was highlighted by activists as offering discursive opportunities that gave visibility and centrality to health rights. The socially and geographically unequal distribution of the consequences of the virus drew attention to health rights and placed them in a global perspective. As a representative of the Third World Network (TWN) told us

> people got outraged ... Many understood that no one is safe until everybody is safe ... So people are dying and then they realise there is something to be done about this. And, in a way, people also realised how the world is unequal, right? Which created a unity among the vulnerable, right? A unity of solidarity among the vulnerable. (interview no. 7)

Baba Aye, the Health and Social Sector Officer of Public Services International (PSI), echoed the sentiment that 'crises are also always ... in one way or the other, opportunities ... It was a moment of opportunity, although a painful one' (interview no. 5). This opportunity offered by the pandemic was evident in the mobilisation of a wide range of organisational networks. In the words of K.M. Gopakumar,

> this was the biggest mobilisation that happened since Doha, after the conclusion of the TRIPS Agreement, this was the biggest mobilisation around this issue [of patents] ... It did raise a lot of awareness, a lot of activism around it ... There have been many civil society organisations working on access to medicines, but you suddenly find the air traffic employees association supporting the waiver, the economists supporting the waiver and local movements supporting the waiver ... I would say that this movement, in a way, touched various constituencies ... It did challenge the patents and it clearly raised the message that nothing is sacrosanct about the patents. (interview no. 7)

Targeting the WTO, the very founder and defender of the TRIPS Agreement, the campaign called for a generalised patent waiver for all Covid-19-related innovations, with the intention of avoiding the time- and energy-consuming disputes that would be involved in developing Compulsory Licensing strategies for each member state and each product. In addition, the waiver was intended to ensure that those countries with little or no manufacturing capacity – and who consequently could not use CLs – would have their fair access to life-saving products.

However, the campaign faced full-frontal opposition launched by Western governments and the pharmaceutical industry. EC Vice-President Vladis Dombrovskis, for example, warned against the waiver proposal, saying that

> [t]he waiver proposed by India and South Africa does not seem to be the appropriate measure as it would undermine the private-public partnerships that have been critical for the rapid development of vaccines and that remain critical for their production. Such a step would also risk limiting incentives for research of the innovative medical products that would need to be developed to respond to new health challenges. (European Parliament, 2020)

The stance taken by the EC Vice-President reflects the relevance and potential of the waiver proposal in its early stages. This is also underlined by the statement issued by the International Federation of Pharmaceutical Manufacturers & Associations (IFPMA) in 2021, which described the waiver as 'an extreme measure for an unidentified problem' that 'leads towards a significant escalation in anti-IP positioning in multilateral fora, with potential consequences around the globe' (IFPIA, 2021). The Federation also highlighted the 'risk that the momentum generated by this proposal [will] create a spillover of an anti-IP narrative to other multilateral fora, and divert attention away from real access challenges worldwide' (ibid.).

It was not until June 2022, when vaccines were widely available in the Global North, that the WTO announced its decision on the proposal put forward by India and South Africa: to allow CLs for the export of Covid-19 vaccines by eligible countries for a period of five years. The organisations involved in the campaign opposed the decision as 'inadequate' and condemned the WTO for taking so long to come to a decision in the midst of the pandemic emergency (Médecins Sans Frontières International, 2022; Oxfam International, 2022). In addition, Médecins Sans Frontières International President Christos Christou criticised the European institutions for their hypocritical and superficial solidarity and expressed his disappointment at their collective inability to reduce the glaring inequalities between the Global North and the Global South. Finally, he called on LMIC governments to use TRIPS flexibilities to push for CLs, IP reform and the production and provision of generic medicines (Médecins Sans Frontières International, 2022).

In what follows, we will trace the international campaign for patent waivers and analyse it in terms of the repertoires of action, organisational networks and frames it mobilised, highlighting the opportunities and challenges of international mobilisation during the pandemic critical juncture.

The Repertoire of Action: Pandemic Challenges Reinforce Path Dependency

As we have argued, transnational campaigns often rely on a combination of insider and outsider strategies, aimed at the specific international organisation(s) that are targeted. In the case of the WTO, patent challengers have historically invested in building strong relationships with national delegations, as well as launching public awareness campaigns. While disruptive contestation has targeted the WTO at various critical moments, the pandemic period severely limited the possibility of engaging in street protests, limiting tactical options such as global days of action or counter-summits. This reluctance to engage in more disruptive forms of protest also resonated with the traditions of the main organisations involved in the waiver campaign. In this section, we will present the repertoire of action mobilised by the campaign, which we will show to be centred on knowledge-building and awareness-raising. Following this, we will discuss some of the strategic limitations as identified by the activists themselves.

Within the general diffusion of the transnational movement for A2M, the pandemic posed specific challenges that to some extent increased the distance from a potential base of grassroots reference. Reflecting on the campaign, one activist told us about the obstacles that one is faced with when 'you move online' (interview no. 7), which may facilitate the widening of the campaign's audience, but does not encourage the creation of strong and lasting relationships and affiliations with A2M.

This 'online turn' further reinforced A2M's focus on lobbying decision-makers and raising public awareness. According to representatives of the TWN, this approach was rooted in the waiver campaign from the very beginning as

> Covid is a manifestation [of how] the existing policies, especially the neoliberal policies have undermined the capability of governments, [of] state[s] to respond effectively to Covid ... by October, India and South Africa filed a patent waiver. So, we suddenly started working on it, we talked to ... organisations, we did briefings, we organised various webinars, sign-on letters, statements ... We wrote a couple of articles. (interview no. 7)

The focus on webinars, statements and articles is linked to A2M's focus on knowledge building. The strategy of the Global Initiative for Economic, Social and Cultural Rights (GI-ESCR), for example, can be summarised as a 'change in narratives at the conceptual level' (interview no. 8). According to its Programme Officer on the Right to Health, the initiative has 'a theory of change [that] rests on [the following] pillars: the conceptual level, evidence, advocacy and change. So, we collect evidence on these conceptual narratives, and then we try to influence policy makers' (ibid.). Knowledge building is crucial given the information asymmetries that underpin the global health scene. As the organisers recounted, most of the deliberations on the waiver were kept secret, while the politicians involved in these procedures at the WTO were usually not sufficiently informed about the issue of patents. As we understand it, A2M's strategy focuses on developing and disseminating expert knowledge to those actors who can make a difference.

While this repertoire was easily adaptable to the constraints on physical forms of protest introduced as a result of the pandemic, it also had some limitations. One of these relates to coordination between the international and national levels. According to Susana Barria, PSI's Global Coordinator for Health Equity, time was of the essence when it came to getting responses to open letters from affiliates spread across the globe, which often delayed the campaign. As she outlined:

> you need to give time even if things move too slow. And at the same time there was a situation where things were also changing and moving fast ... So, there were different rhythms that we had to adjust to: the rhythm of what we can do on the ground, and the rhythm of the campaign, of the activism happening with civil society. So, there were different dynamics that needed to be brought together at some point. And sometimes, for instance, we told our affiliates [if you don't] sign in three days, it's not going to happen. We cannot! We have much slower processes. (interview no. 4)

The focus of the campaign on funded projects raised criticism from some members of the coalition involved in promoting it. As one activist with extensive experience in A2M activism noted,

> [w]e changed what victory means. We changed what results mean. When you're talking about results, and I ask you 'what were the results of our organisation last year?', you say 'look five publications, five reports and two webinars and three meetings in Geneva' ... This is part of changing the narrative. But it's not by chance; when you are filling out a report to your donor, [you have come to] call it a result. How many papers you've published. This is a result. So, I think this new talk, this new way of talking, is part of a game. (interview no. 6)

The sum of these critiques culminates in a rejection of the 'reactive mode' of A2M, as '[s]omething appears, and we go after it; something else appears and we go after [that]. And suddenly our positions are always determined by the other side' (ibid.). This reactive mode reinforces the adaptation of social movement organisations to the limits set by institutions and increases their distance from their constituencies.

Moreover, according to our interlocutors, the repertoire of action is also limited by the dependence on donors. As critically observed by activists, dependence on donors forces some more structured CSOs to adapt to their institutional logic. As one activist told us,

> [w]e cannot underestimate the importance of donors ... Because they have a button, I mean the Open Society Foundation [OSF] and UNIDAID, and a couple of others, [the] Ford Foundation etc. They can just press a button at anytime and then everything is off ... If we are serious about our work we should be asking ourselves 'ok, if they don't believe in what we believe, why are they funding us?'... In my opinion, it is clear: because we are not dangerous enough. So it's cool, it's cool to finance some organisations that are legitimising the terrible and incredible process of listening to us for

> 1 minute. Such as at the WHO. It's crazy! So they give us the money to go to Geneva and we go there and we deliver a speech and then in the end we lose, because we know we are going to lose, but in the end we say at least they heard us, at least we brought the voices from the South and the people who suffer, to the place where they are making decisions and everyone is happy again. (ibid.)

The lack of a clear critique of power imbalances in the global health arena is then understood as a 'reactive mode', which leads A2M to seek a 'good argument' capable of sensitising and persuading through 'reasonable demands'.

This strategy also relies on communication skills that, on reflection, our interlocutors stated they lacked. According to them, most of the social movements and CSOs involved in the campaign lacked digital media skills and a connection to their constituencies. The pandemic exacerbated this disconnect by reinforcing tactical choices such as open letters, which tend to appeal to concerned individuals but rarely reach the most affected constituencies.

Covid-19, therefore, further highlighted the stalemate at the heart of A2M, prompting activists to reflect on the need to redefine their strategies and reconfigure their tactics. In a conversation with a critical member of A2M, they asked themselves, '[w]hat's *my* solution? To go back to the local level, see what people need and fight for these needs. To have real victories again' (ibid.; emphasis added).

In sum, anti-contagion measures increasingly reinforced insider strategies, which were seen as incapable of mobilising the rank and file to use protest as a form of pressure.

Organisational Network: Coalition Building around the Waiver

These strategic challenges were also linked to the heterogeneity of the broad milieus mobilised during the pandemic critical juncture. As we have argued, the pandemic allowed attention to be focused on health issues, facilitating the convergence of a wide variety of CSOs well beyond those more directly concerned with health rights. Concerns about free and equitable access to vaccines became a central demand around which organisations working on health rights – but also on human rights, development, labour and gender issues – converged as part of a loose network, particularly at the transnational level. In this section, we will look at the ways in which networking proved successful, but also at some of its limitations in terms of mobilising capacity.

As is common in transnational campaigns, the organisational structures were based on loose coordination or networks of networks of very different organisations. One major ad-hoc umbrella coalition that formed during the pandemic is the People's Medicines Alliance, 'a coalition of over 100 organizations and networks, supported by Nobel Laureates, health experts, economists, Heads of States, faith leaders and activists, working together towards equitable access to medical technologies that help to prevent and respond to COVID-19 and future pandemics' (People's Medicines Alliance, n.d.).

The Alliance grew organically out of the May 2020 Open Letter for a People's Vaccine, organised under the slogan 'We work together to end vaccine apartheid'. It included major civil society organisations such as Oxfam, Save the Children and ActionAid; fair trade and manufacturing campaigns; human rights organisations such as Amnesty International and Human Rights Watch; as well as trade union organisations such as the International Trade Union Confederation (ITUC), PSI, UNI Global Union, UNITE and the International Transport Workers' Federation (ITF). At the core of the network are a large number of well-established CSOs such as Doctors for Vaccine Equity (DVE), PHM, Physicians for Human Rights, *Salud Por Derecho*, STOPAIDS, UNAIDS and Universities Allied for Essential Medicines.

The organisational structure was characterised by loose coordination. By way of illustration, PHM, one of the most active groups in the coalition, describes itself as:

> a network of networks, organisations and individuals with some centrally supported programs.... As a movement, we do not follow rigid structures, but broadly speaking PHM is structured as follows: On country level, PHM manifest in the form of groups coming together nationally or locally. Country circles or sometimes called 'local chapters' grow according to the country's need; they are most often loose networks which come together for joint action around specific issues, but can be formalised and legalised as an organisation. There is no set way on how PHM organises locally as this depends on the local context, chosen activities and the circumstances of the people building PHM. Regionally, PHM aims to build coalitions and networks to encourage support, sharing and learning.... The way each region coordinates itself, is defined by the needs and context of the region. Centrally PHM aims to employ regional coordinators for each region. So far only Africa and the Middle East Regions have such coordinator. Each PHM region is represented in the Global Steering Council. (People's Health Movement, n.d.)

While global A2M networks tend to have positive, lasting effects in terms of confidence-building, internal divergences are also evident. The diversity of the network was undoubtedly empowering, and it allowed the campaign to 'catch on like wildfire' (interview no. 7). Indeed, as Susanna Barria noted, 'despite the fact that A2M was central it wasn't alone. Feminist groups also jumped in, the trade union movement jumped in' (interview no. 4). However, as she continued, they jumped in from their different reference points. So, I think that this aggregation of movements also meant a more powerful campaign, overall. But it's like a campaign with many campaigns. Or many families of political actors that ... some of them have some shared history and some just do not. (ibid.)

Indeed, tensions emerged between groups according to their main areas of intervention (for example, between trade unions and organisations involved in international forms of solidarity), but also, as is often the case in transnational campaigns, between the better structured and larger civil society organisations and the smaller, grassroots ones. Returning to the earlier discussion, the professionalisation of the largest CSOs was seen by some as a key problem, as it led to a disconnect with their constituencies, who no longer felt represented. One activist told us about the gap between the advocacy work carried out by CSOs and the constituencies they are supposed to represent, highlighting the contrast between the slow pace of the organisations and the pressing and immediate needs of most of the constituencies that A2M mobilises for:

[w]e, as an NGO and as a movement, are not the people who suffer from the lack of access to essential medicines. So for us it's too easy to say 'oh, it's what we can do, or it's what's possible.' It's too easy because we're so detached from the people ... We should first of all go back to our basis because even what we call grassroots is not grassroots. (interview no. 6)

Finally, the coalition suffered from tensions between groups rooted in the Global North and those rooted in the Global South. As we have argued in Section 3, divisions arose either from vested interests in supporting the domestic pharmaceutical industry in certain HICs, or from a lack of attention to access elsewhere once vaccines were introduced in HICs.

Collective Framing: Thinking Small or Thinking Big?

In order to understand the evolution of the international campaign for free access to vaccines, it is important to look at the framing opportunities that were open to the campaign during this period. However, as we shall show, the acceptance of the patent system challenged these opportunities, as 'solutionist' and pragmatic frames prevailed over more contentious ones.

In general, the need to justify the request for a waiver is linked to the health emergency and the utilitarian need for global vaccination to achieve global herd immunity. However, these pragmatic frames were also linked to the justice frames that are so powerful in HSMs. For example, in the open letter in support of the waiver, which was signed by 400 CSOs, the demand for the waiver is framed in terms of both efficacy and justice:

> When COVID-19 was declared to be a pandemic, there was overwhelming consensus that to curb the spread of COVID-19, there was an urgent need for international collaboration to speed up product development, scale up of manufacturing, expand the supply of effective medical technologies and ensure everyone, everywhere is protected. There were even calls including from several Heads of State for COVID-19 medical products to be treated as global public goods. Seven months into the pandemic, there is no meaningful global policy solution to ensure access. Instead, there is an inequality of access to critical technologies that are needed to address the pandemic. Many countries, especially developing and least developed countries struggling to contain COVID-19 have experienced and are facing acute shortages of medical products, including access to diagnostic testing. Furthermore, wealthy nations representing only 13 percent of the global population have locked up at least half the doses of the world's five leading potential vaccines. (Médecins Sans Frontières Access Campaign, 2020a)

Responsibility for the inequitable and inefficient distribution of vaccines and medicines is attributed to the pharmaceutical industry and its driving motives of profit maximisation, which obstructs the development of a comprehensive global health strategy through opaque negotiations and deals. The letter continues:

> [i]n this pandemic, the pharmaceutical industry has mainly pursued 'business as usual' approaches, entrenching monopolistic intellectual property (IP) controls over COVID-19 health technologies that restrict scale-up of manufacturing, lock out diversified suppliers, and undermine competition that results in lower prices ... The COVID-19 Technology Access Pool (C-TAP) launched by WHO (to voluntarily share knowledge, IP and data), has been rejected by the pharmaceutical industry. Instead, companies continue to sign secretive and restrictive licensing agreements ... [E]merging intellectual property infringement disputes on COVID-19 technologies threatens to block collaborative research and development and manufacturing of COVID-19 medical products. These restrictive business strategies have directly translated into exorbitant pricing and profiteering. (ibid.)

The letter also highlights the fact that the financial burden of the pandemic on health systems and economies will prevent many countries from affording expensive medical products, while intellectual property and technology barriers – if not addressed globally – will limit access to new treatments and vaccines, hindering both public health and economic recovery.

The main argument for the need for a global solution is also supported by the petition (signed by almost one million citizens) to the WTO, the CEOs of pharmaceutical companies, all WTO member countries and the G7 leaders for a waiver to 'ensure access to lifesaving COVID-19 vaccines, treatments and equipment for everyone in the world' because '[t]he pandemic will not be over, until it's over everywhere' (World Trade Organisation, 2020).

The call for a waiver is linked to the need for global political solutions. According to Progressive International, '[t]his crisis has revealed the urgent and enduring need for international coordination, cooperation, and solidarity: no country can end the pandemic alone' (Progressive International, 2020). Similarly, the ITUC stigmatised what it termed 'vaccine nationalism' and pointed to international cooperation as the only solution because 'the moral imperative to provide vaccinations to all people in the world is underpinned by the public health need to suppress the virus in every part of the world' (International Trade Union Confederation, 2021). This would include

> government-led initiatives to ramp up production of approved vaccines and continue development of new vaccines; removal of intellectual property barriers, including the implementation TRIPS waivers and measures to stop price-gouging on vaccines, tests and treatments; further investment in COVAX; accelerated support for production capacity in developing countries to meet the needs of this and future pandemics [as well as] investment in health and other public services to ensure vaccines can be distributed and given efficiently, and investment in social protection. (ibid.)

In addition to these appeals for effectiveness and equity, and in line with the ECI campaign, the organisers of the patent waiver campaign also highlighted the role of the public sector and funding in vaccine development, as well as frequently published data on the private appropriation of public knowledge during the health emergency (Oxfam International, 2020). As Susana Barria noted, PSI 'had a language of vaccines being a public good themselves, [highlighting] the role that public financing played in all of this' (interview no. 4). In addition, at both the national and transnational levels, trade unions attempted to bridge health rights and justice frames to labour rights and public goods, as it is

> the workers that produce public things, that produce things that are essential and we believe that to have quality, universal and ensured realisation of rights they actually need to be linked with a public interest and for that thing to be public goods and very often that means not only in public hands but also with elements of democratic oversight. (ibid.)

International trade union federations linked these demands to a broader critique of the management of the pandemic, which was seen as an opportunity to further promote private sector profits at the expense of workers. National unions were therefore encouraged to contact their own national governments 'to ensure they are aware that health workers and other public services workers expect them to support these proposals', and to stress the importance of 'occupational health and safety, work re-organisation, social distancing, ventilation, masks, and a massive increase in testing' (International Trade Union Confederation, 2021).

In a similar vein, IndustriALL Global Union put forward a critique that linked health rights to the 'challenge of the fundamentals of the world's social, political and economic security' posed by the pandemic. In this environment, as the health crisis gradually turned into an economic crisis, they argued that

> [a]ccess to affordable medicines, tools, vaccines, diagnostics and treatment for Covid-19 is paramount for a recovery from the crisis. No one should be left behind and no one is safe until everyone is protected. (IndustriALL Global Union, 2020)

For their part, development organisations presented the waiver as a way to fight poverty. For example, the Drugs for Neglected Diseases Initiative (DNDi), a core member of A2M, saw the campaign as a continuation of its long and persistent fight for access, 'to ensure that all people – including the poorest, most vulnerable, and those at highest risk – are guaranteed timely and equitable access to the fruits of scientific progress in this pandemic' (DNDi, 2020). The pandemic has also reignited critiques of the unequal distribution of burdens – such as disease and poverty – across the globe, and in 2022 civil society turned to the WTO to highlight how

> [t]he crisis has been exacerbated and continues to adversely affect many developing and least developed countries as promises of solidarity and collaboration towards equitable access to vaccines, treatments and tests have mostly failed to materialise. (People's Health Movement et al., 2022)

In addition, NGOs mobilised human rights in the campaign for the waiver. In its efforts to lobby WTO member states, Amnesty International appealed that

> COVID-19 is not only a health and economic, but also a human rights crisis ... The World Health Assembly has recognized the role of extensive immunization against COVID-19 as a global public good for health in preventing, containing and stopping transmission in order to bring the pandemic to an end, once safe, quality, efficacious, effective, accessible and affordable vaccines are available. (Amnesty International, 2020)

Networks such as PHM and the People's Medicine Alliance converged on a social justice framework. According to the latter's Five Point Plan for a People's Vaccine,

> [t]he world is facing a vaccine apartheid – billions of people are unprotected facing the threat of illness and death from this cruel disease. Billions are also facing hunger and destitution as a result of lockdowns and continued economic hardship. Billions are facing the huge social impacts, including children who have missed many months of education and women having faced increased domestic violence and many more hours of unpaid care work. Insufficient vaccine supply combined with rich country hoarding of doses mean most people in developing countries face this killer disease with minimal access to protection. (People's Medicines Alliance, 2022)

While bridging the call for the waiver with frames resonant with the core concerns of different organisations allows for coalition building, there are challenges related to the diversity of positions contained within such a coalition, which precludes broader reflections on the very definition of health and care and normalises the uncritical acceptance of medicalising trends. As Nicoletta Dentico explained:

> [f]or me, the A2M has always been [about] the Alma-Ata vision, the primary healthcare vision where medicines are one of the many other elements for [the] implementation of the right to health, ok? So, I've always been an advocate for access to medicines, but I've been also trying to insert the access to medicines in the broader picture of health systems. Which is actually something that has always made me rather confrontational towards all these mechanisms like the Global Fund, you know this financing mechanism that was primarily focusing on the drug and only later, after many years they entered into [the discussion regarding] healthcare systems. (interview no. 1)

Sections of A2M also expressed concerns about framing access as an issue that only affects LMICs, when similar challenges related to health rights have also recently become an issue for HICs. Again in Dentico's words,

> at the time we had Hepatitis C, which was more a case that hit the [Global] North! Of course it also hit India [and] other countries ... But it hit the North! That was in a way the self-fulfilling prophecies [we had] thirty years, fifteen years earlier that this [IP reform] was not [only a problem of LMICs]. (ibid.)

More broadly, the main criticism of A2M's stance centred on its acceptance of the TRIPS framework, which stigmatised patents as a strategic constraint, implying that the rules of the game should be accepted rather than challenged fundamentally. According to Alan Rossi Silva, this represents a departure from the core values on which the A2M movement was built:

> I would say that we cannot call ourselves anymore anti-patent movement ... We said 'look the whole debate must now be framed between two extremes'. One is TRIPS-Plus rules and a lot of bizarre demands from the Global North and transnational corporations related to IP, and on the other side, the other

The Contentious Politics of Global Health Movements 53

> extreme is precisely TRIPS flexibilities. And then we accepted this framework ... and there is no battle within this framework. Because we lost. (interview no. 6)

A2M's focus on and prioritisation of immediate solutions was also seen as a constraint for CSOs, especially as these are increasingly difficult to enact and implement. Thus, the partial success of the movement in securing VLs at the end of the WTO deliberations was seen as yet another compromise that, instead of increasing opportunities and space for challenges to patents, actually increased the leverage of the pharmaceutical industry. This is

> [b]ecause it was so complicated, ... to focus on Voluntary Licenses and the Patent Pool, which is [also] based on Voluntary Licenses. It's an arena, a place, an organisation where we basically say 'ok, let's not be confrontational, let's try to cooperate, we're going to be good with you Big Pharma, we're going to share some of this knowledge and we're going to work within this context and we will find a kind of mediation point where we can together, represent the break that we want to see'. So, that has worked of course, it has worked, it has produced drugs, but at the same time it has created a political culture of pragmatism, of solutionism. That has skewed the conversation towards Voluntary Licenses rather than Compulsory Licenses. So it has not densified the little room for manoeuvre that the government had, but actually shifted all the mediation into this new entity situated at the WHO, yes, but it's all based on the good will of the pharmaceutical companies. (ibid.)

This dominant pragmatic view is seen as weakening the challenge to the commodification of health, since, in the view of critical activists, the strategies of some A2M campaigns are dictated by the logic of the market, incorporating concepts such as 'consumers' and adhering to the discourse of 'market incentives', rather than imagining political solutions to access problems. Indeed, pragmatism is seen as limiting the ability to imagine scenarios in which intellectual property rights are lifted, while fundamentally undermining the role that the public sector could play in developing a more sustainable system of public health and pharmaceutical innovation. According to one of our interviewees,

> we don't seem to be able to design another scenario, imagine another scenario. [We cannot think of] the role of the public sector and the fact that certain drugs, at least some, should not be covered by IP. They should be exempted, as they have been for a long time. There's a reason why this type of health-related innovation should not be patented. You [need to] de-commodify it, de-financialise it, and restitute it back [to] where it belongs: the health domain. Which includes industry but it should have a public health and state-owned agenda. Where companies can participate, but

under the conditions that the government [and] the public sector sets for them. (interview no. 1)

As part of a broader critique, some of our interviewees aired their concerns about the increasing penetration of 'humanitarian' frames within A2M, which is seen as contributing to the privatisation of global health governance. As one DNDi activist put it,

> [s]o you don't only have the Medicines Patent Pool but Medicine Malaria Venture, Global Fund, UNAID, Fund for Diagnostics, Drugs for Neglected Diseases Initiative ... all this mushrooming of combination of public support and competence and the private support and capacity to produce, which originated in entities that *de facto* are all private entities, they are all entities of private law, and in a way they have contributed to de-responsibilising governments, they have divided the global health arena according to diseases basically, infectious, neglected, tropical. (interview no. 1)

We understand, then, that while the critical juncture of the pandemic opened up discursive opportunities for patent contestation over the period, it also posed a number of challenges. The pandemic undoubtedly opened up the debate on patents for health-related products and innovations, problematising the former and broadening the audience of those contesting their use. However, the pragmatic focus of the campaign on immediate solutions, combined with the challenges inherent in communicating intellectual property as a legal entity with health implications, multiplied the difficulties in articulating and disseminating criticisms of the patent regime. Ultimately, the unyielding stance of the pharmaceutical industry, which was strongly represented at the highest levels of power, effectively resulted in the reversal of established narratives regarding health rights and the right to health, leading to the consolidation and advancement of humanitarian approaches to global health.

Conclusion

In this section, we have followed the intensification of transnational connections between health movements and health rights groups, as prompted by the health emergency. We have shown how global health governance and the lack of accountability and transparency that characterises it offered a ground for the multiplication and proliferation of anti-patent contestation on a world scale. An upward scale shift of protests followed the perception of the increasing competences of international organisations, especially those able to affect trade and patents (Boli and Thomas 1999; della Porta, Kriesi and Rucht 1999; della Porta and Tarrow 2005; Smith et al. 1994).

Following the announcement of the decision on patents for Covid-19 vaccines in developing countries at the 12th Ministerial Conference in June 2022, the organisers of the Patent Waiver Campaign openly opposed the deal, attributing responsibility to the HIC that initially blocked the proposal and subsequently modified it, two years after its submission. In the words of Max Lawson, Co-Chair of the People's Vaccine Alliance and Head of Inequality Policy at Oxfam, the conduct of wealthy countries at the WTO,

> has been utterly shameful. The EU has blocked anything that resembles a meaningful intellectual property waiver. The UK and Switzerland have used negotiations to twist the knife and make any text even worse. And the US has sat silently in negotiations with red lines designed to limit the impact of any agreement. (Oxfam International, 2020)

Nevertheless, the campaign was perceived as having achieved some degree of success by certain activists, largely due to the impact it has had on fostering a critical perspective and an understanding of the future implications. On a positive note, Baba Aye informed us that despite the WTO decision being 'not even a shadow of what we wanted', it did result in a qualitative change within and beyond PSI, particularly in terms of the visibility of patent contestation. He asserted that the campaign

> made our work in international tax and trade much more powerful ... Just a handful of persons were more likely to be specialists in the headquarters of our unions. And knew nearly anything about TRIPS or knew nothing about how trade rules could devastatingly impact on the health and well-being of their colleagues and the members of their families! ... I saw a major shift not only in the knowledge of what TRIPS is and what international trade and tax amounts to, but also an appreciation of the need to change this ... Because there are [moments where] international struggles related to the TRIPS waiver and maybe even beyond, to international tax and trade, are thrown up by history. And we are coming out to fight. We won't be starting where we started from in 2020. We'll be building on a solid, you know, pinnacle that this work brought. (int. no. 5)

A similar viewpoint is espoused by TWN, another pivotal entity within the A2M network. As K.M. Gopakumar observed,

> one of the positive things is that the countries came forward and raised this issue. The waiver proposal itself is a positive thing. Because it challenges the so-called sacrosanct façade of the TRIPS agreement, right? So this in itself. And around 70 [countries] came together at different points in time and challenged the agreement, with the waiver proposal. So ... that itself is a good sign. So but we didn't get the optimal result. I would say two [positive] things: one is that countries had the courage to challenge the

agreement. That conveys a message that this is a problem. Then the second is that a lot of social mobilisation happened around this. Even in the North, more in the North than the South ...That shows that there is much room for resonance now, that there is much more, people are ready to talk about this but of course things might die down, memory is short so ... But still if you look at it, these are the two positive outcomes of the campaign ... People will raise this issue when access is limited in other situations, other diseases. And there would be opportunity for further mobilisation ... They will take the lessons, and some incremental benefits will come, people will know there is this issue to be addressed. (int. no. 7)

In light of these insights, reflections and frustrations, A2M shifted its focus and efforts towards the ongoing proceedings of the WHO's Pandemic Prevention, Preparedness, and Response Accord. Following the critical juncture of the pandemic and the related opportunity to operate 'outside the four walls of the WTO' (int. no. 6), A2M appears to be returning to the four walls of the WHO, the forum that is most proximate to the movement and most distant from impactful decision-making and policymaking.

5 Transnational Protests for Access to Medicines: Some Conclusions

This Element presents the conclusions of our analysis of two transnational protest campaigns for access to vaccines and treatments related to Covid-19 during the pandemic. This specific moment has been identified within the broader context of the long-standing interactions between Health Social Movements and public health institutions, focusing on the transnational dimension of protest for health rights. As decisions pertaining to public health have increasingly been made at the international and transnational levels, collective actors advocating for access to health as a human right have begun to engage with international organisations and transnational institutions, adapting their approach to align with the unique characteristics of each entity. Our analysis is grounded in the field of social movement studies, with the aim of elucidating the manner in which international and transnational political opportunities influence the tactics, organisational structures and framing of social movements. In this concluding section, we will consider the broader implications of our empirical analysis for the study of Health Social Movements on the international and transnational levels.

The research on transnational protest has indicated that social movements play a pivotal role in establishing and disseminating a normative framework on health rights. Research on civil society in global health has highlighted the significance of collaboration with international organisations for the purposes of both agenda-setting and the implementation of health policies. The human rights framework has been employed consistently by organisations such as ActionAid, MSF, Oxfam and Save the Children in the promotion of health rights (Noh, 2024). With some institutional acknowledgement, medicines and vaccines have been presented as public goods, and calls for compliance with general norms have been used to legitimise intervention in all decisions affecting health (including, for example, water privatisation and the need to invest in public health infrastructure) (ibid.; Mercer et al., 2014).

This process of institutional recognition has presented a series of challenges for the mobilisation of health rights. Biehl (2007) has observed that in the context of HIV/AIDS activism in Brazil, for example, as activists became increasingly involved in the management of substantial funds and government advisory roles, they gradually lost touch with grassroots mobilisation. Concurrently, the transfer of decision-making authority to international organisations with a focus on trade and property rights has resulted in significant constraints regarding access. This has been particularly evident in the case of the WTO, which is perceived as being highly secretive and hostile towards external parties, particularly in relation to CSOs (Hopewell, 2015; Steffek, 2012).

The selective approach of the WTO in granting access to external parties has resulted in a tendency towards conformity and depoliticisation among CSOs seeking to engage with the organisation. The WTO's selectivity in granting access to outsiders has had effects in terms of the increased conformism and depoliticisation of CSOs that wish to intervene therein. Relevant scholarship has suggested that

> in the process of seeking to transform the WTO, many civil society actors have themselves been transformed: they have become more technocratic and increasingly moved towards advocating positions that accord with the dominant neoliberal trade paradigm. (Azedi & Schofer, 2023)

This Element serves to corroborate these trends. Following the signing of the TRIPS Agreement, activists concerned with access to medicines invested in the formation of alliances – primarily with states – and in the construction of knowledge (see also Murphy-Gregory, 2012). As has been demonstrated here, the limited instances of partial success on the part of A2M activists (see Nattrass, 2015, for an analysis of the ambiguity of the Doha Declaration) frequently resulted in the acceptance and tacit legitimisation of the existing patent regime.

Furthermore, our analysis has indicated that the adoption of technocratic standards and bureaucratic models by some of these organisations has resulted in a fragmentation of the protest field, with more resourced groups becoming increasingly distanced from the grassroots (Hopewell, 2015; Williams & Ford,

1999). The specific national opportunities also gave rise to internal tensions when organising at the transnational level (Smith et al., 1994), resulting in a division of the movement between Geneva-based civil society organisations in the Global North and those based in the Global South. Additionally, tensions have emerged between the transnational advocacy logic and the grassroots contentious politics of the national and local levels.

In contrast to the WTO, the European Union is widely regarded as being endowed with a higher degree of democratic accountability and with mechanisms that are specifically designed with the intention of involving civil society organisations (CSOs) and expanding citizen participation. However, recent research has observed an increasing tendency towards technocratic arguments, as well as a transfer of decision-making authority from the more accountable European Parliament to the less transparent European Commission. While scholarship has demonstrated this shift since the 2008 financial crisis, which saw the advancement of the European Central Bank as well as Ecofin (della Porta & Parks, 2018), the outbreak of the Covid-19 pandemic served to reinforce this trend. In particular, the pandemic crisis witnessed a concentration of decision-making authority in the President of the European Commission, accompanied by a notable lack of transparency regarding decision-making processes (Christou & della Porta, 2024; della Porta et al., 2022; Müller et al., 2022).

Generally speaking, there have been few instances in which protest campaigns have been able to facilitate a convergence of the various groups and networks. As issues assume an increasingly global character, progressive social movements have not only contested the politics and policies of the EU, but also the very borders of the EU polity and the rationale for its existence. This has contributed to the growth of critical Europeanism, which has sought to establish connections between struggles beyond the EU and to target other international organisations. In addressing this challenge, EU civil society organisations have encountered strategic dilemmas that have frequently intensified internal divisions, thereby rendering the initiation of transnational campaigns within and beyond the EU a more arduous process. As we show here, the Europeanisation of health governance further prompted the transnationalisation of anti-patent contestation over the course of the health emergency.

Furthermore, our research has corroborated the findings that the selective inclusion of CSOs practiced by the EU has had a taming effect (Kaldor, 2003). It is evident that the contentious politics of the pandemic were characterised by a high level of tension. Despite the considerable efforts and resources invested in advocacy and participation, it proved impossible to achieve policy change towards universal and free access to Covid-19 vaccines. Our analysis has demonstrated that firms and economic interests possessed a considerable advantage within an international system that was dominated by market liberalisation norms. The emphasis placed on human rights norms by social movements converging was readily eclipsed by the influence of robust economic interests, which shaped the actions of both Member States and international organisations. The assumption that international organisations would serve as deliberative arenas proved erroneous, as even the most fundamental human right during the pandemic – access to vaccines and medicine – was subordinated to a profit logic.

As the activists we interviewed indicated, the very hope that the global nature of the pandemic would provide discursive opportunities for global access to medicines failed to materialise, due to the nationalism attitudes displayed by the most powerful states and the greed of the pharmaceutical industry. While the pandemic undoubtedly prompted a re-evaluation of access as a human right (Buckland-Merrett et al., 2017), social movement activists involved in the 'No Profit on Pandemic' campaign ultimately characterised the emergency situation as 'bittersweet'. As one of the activists elucidated, the pandemic

> created opportunities for health to be more at the center. And I think civil society managed to create a lot of mobilisation. So, in certain ways it was a success because it made health more popular and it created momentum for health to [advance as central] and to have more financial resources from donors investing in health, which is fundamental, we cannot work without money ... But at the same time, unfortunately, it also created a lot of space for private actors to become more and more involved in health ... it really showed, as in the HIV crisis, how there's a problem with corporate power of pharmaceutical companies. So, bittersweet in terms of narrative success, but also in terms of concrete power, if you look at the Pandemic Treaty once again is quite influenced by corporate power. (interview no. 8)

Despite the failure to bring about a patent waiver, the activists were able to identify some positive outcomes resulting from their efforts. The global health crisis, accompanied by a significant rise in inequality, has placed the issue of rights at the forefront of the political and social discourse. Among the outcomes of this process were the acquisition of symbolic and practical meaning for health rights, which served to bridge various claims and existing struggles. The health movements, which had traditionally been quite fragmented, experienced growth among health workers and patients alike.

The advent of the Covid-19 pandemic prompted a period of introspection within the A2M milieu. A preliminary reflection addressed the necessity to engage the most affected constituencies. Indeed, the history of the A2M movement demonstrates that successful campaigns require the involvement of affected populations in contentious politics. This has an impact on the range of available actions, the organisational structure and the processes of collective framing. With regard to the forms of action, the most successful campaigns have combined lobbying, petitions and litigation with protest action. This was not the case during the period under examination, despite the mobilisation on health rights by workers in the health system, as well as patients and citizens more widely. However, when anti-patent slogans and banners were displayed at demonstrations, which were themselves subject to restrictions due to the lockdown measures, they were not explicitly associated with A2M. Rather, they were shared among broader and well-established movement networks. As Nicoletta Dentico outlined in relation to the European branch of A2M, the pandemic made the lack of a grassroots movement a visible problem. She lamented the absence of this level, saying that

> [w]e don't have social movements, we don't have the indigenous populations as you have in FAO[7] for example, or elsewhere. You don't have the people from the communities. They don't belong to this thing. And we have the assumption that we represent them. This is not true. (interview no. 1)

Connecting insider and outsider strategies is acknowledged as an important task in the future. This is connected to the advancement of health rights as a unifying framework. Those contesting patents over the course of the pandemic frequently invoked the frame of human rights, most often approached through humanitarian narratives. As evidenced by the case of South Africa's Treatment Action Campaign (TAC) in the 1990s, the defence of the right to health must be linked to wider issues of socio-economic justice. This approach enabled TAC to expand the number of individuals involved in the campaign, as well as the common understanding of what constitutes health. It also served to advance the campaign's claims (Heywood, 2009). Furthermore, the involvement of those communities most affected by the virus and the problems of access to therapeutics created by the IP system were identified as central explanatory factors for the success of both TAC and ACT-UP, although this success was partial.

More broadly, the organisational cleavages that were observed have been linked with the aforementioned co-optation of many organisations within the patent regime, which are often considered to be a given. In the campaigns under examination, the arguments were constructed in a way that combined moral justifications with more pragmatic considerations regarding the resolution of the global health and economic crises. In particular, they reaffirmed the concept

---

[7] UN Food and Agriculture Organisation.

of health as a fundamental human right, as it is typically framed by the A2M movement. Additionally, they employed a more radical and innovative stigmatisation of the 'health apartheid', a term that they used to describe the exclusion of LMICs from the management of the pandemic. The perceived failure of the most pragmatic frames prompted activists to recognise the necessity of responding to the global character of the pandemic through globally interconnected struggles. The distinction between the Global North and the Global South became particularly apparent during the course of the pandemic, as evidenced by the demands and trajectory of the 'No Profit on Pandemic' campaign. In particular, while the ECI only partly addressed the issue of access to medicines, placing it alongside concerns about transparency, public knowledge and the profiteering activities of the pharmaceutical industry, the Indian and South African waiver proposal made a clear argument about the disproportionate impact of the pandemic in LMICs. It called for global solidarity in sharing knowledge, spreading and scaling up production in order to better respond to the pandemic. These profound cleavages within the A2M coalition ultimately undermined the efficacy of the movement.

While the A2M campaigns were able to raise public awareness and gain the support of institutional allies, the studies presented in this Element ultimately resulted in only minimal concessions from the pharmaceutical industry. The failure to achieve the objective of a patent waiver on products and technologies related to Covid-19 can be attributed to the multifaceted nature of the political arena in which diverse actors were involved. It is evident that the transnational campaigns for access to medicines also served to illustrate the strength of the opposition. The pandemic served to accentuate the principal issues inherent to the patent regime. A2M was undermined by the bio-financialisation of pharmaceuticals, which entailed a shift from industrial to financial pharma, as well as the development of the biotech industry. This was due to the fact that HICs encountered difficulties and thus began advocating for their own access to medicines. The rapid developments that took place during the pandemic, including the development of vaccines and their subsequent rollout, also created challenges for the campaign, namely by affecting the resonance of some arguments and further dividing the Global North from the Global South. Consequently, although the global spread of the virus initially appeared to justify calls for global solidarity, once the European population was offered rapid and effective vaccinations, the campaign's framing had to adapt to new developments, including the arrival of vaccines. In light of these experiences and related frustrations, segments of A2M redirected their energies and attention to the proceedings of the WHO's Pandemic Prevention, Preparedness and Response Agreement, which is still in progress.

Abbreviations

A2M	Access to Medicines
APA	Advanced Purchase Agreement
COVAX	Covid-19 Vaccines Global Access
CSO	Civil Society Organisation
DNDi	Drugs for Neglected Diseases initiative
EC	European Commission
ECI	European Citizens' Initiative
EFPIA	European Federation of Pharmaceutical Industries and Associations
EMA	European Medicines Agency
EP	European Parliament
EU	European Union
IFPMA	International Federation of Pharmaceutical Manufacturers and Associations
ITUC	International Trade Union Confederation
MSF	Médecins Sans Frontières
PHM	People's Health Movement
PSI	Public Services International
TRIPS Agreement	Trade-Related Aspects of Intellectual Property Rights' Agreement
TWN	Third World Network
WHO	World Health Organization
WTO	World Trade Organization

Interviews Cited

Alan Rossi Silva: PHM Europe and International Affairs Coordinator of the Brazilian Interdisciplinary AIDS Association.

Alberto Zoratti: Local organiser for Società della Cura.

Ana Vračar: Regional coordinator of PHM Europe and Co-Chair of the PHM steering council.

Baba Aye: PSI Health and Social Sector Officer.

Julie Steendam: PHM Europe and Coordinator of ECI campaign.

K.M. Gopakumar: TWN legal advisor and senior researcher.

Nicoletta Dentico: Head of Global Health programme of Society for International Development (SID) and Co-Chair of Geneva Global Health Hub.

Rossella De Falco: Program Officer on the Right to Health, Global Initiative for Economic, Social and Cultural Rights.

Susana Barria: PSI Sub-regional Secretary for the Andean Sub-region, Colombia and Global Coordinator for Health Equity

References

Abbott, F. M. (2011). The Doha declaration on the TRIPS agreement and public health and the contradictory trend in bilateral and regional free trade agreements (SSRN Scholarly Paper 1977300). https://papers.ssrn.com/abstract=1977300.

Amnesty International. (2020, November). Briefing for WTO member states on the TRIPS waiver proposal for the prevention, containment and treatment of COVID-19. Amnesty International. www.amnesty.org/en/documents/ior40/3365/2020/en/.

Azedi, A., & Schofer, E. (2023). Assessing the anti-globalization movement: Protest against the WTO, IMF, and World Bank in cross-national perspective. The Sociological Quarterly, 64(3), 445–470. https://doi.org/10.1080/00380253.2023.2167672.

Baker, B. K. (2018). A sliver of hope: Analyzing voluntary licenses to accelerate affordable access to medicines (SSRN Scholarly Paper 3123108). https://papers.ssrn.com/abstract=3123108.

Baker, B. K. (2020). Access to medicines activism: Collaboration, conflicts, and complementarities (SSRN Scholarly Paper 3538270). https://papers.ssrn.com/abstract=3538270.

Banaszak-Holl, J., Levitsky, S., & Zald, M. N. (2010). Social Movements and the Transformation of American Health Care. Oxford University Press.

Barone, A. (2024). Repertoires of action and collective memory: The re-emergence of feminist self-managed health centers in Italy. Social Movement Studies. www.academia.edu/122056651/Repertoires_of_action_and_collective_memory_the_re_emergence_of_feminist_self_managed_health_centers_in_Italy.

Biehl, J. G. (2007). Will to Live: AIDS Therapies and the Politics of Survival. Princeton University Press.

Birch, K., & Muniesa, F. (Eds.). (2020). Assetization: Turning Things into Assets in Technoscientific Capitalism. The MIT Press. https://doi.org/10.7551/mitpress/12075.001.0001.

Boin, A., & Rhinard, M. (2023). Crisis management performance and the European Union: The case of COVID-19. *Journal of European Public Policy*, *30*(4), 655–675. https://doi.org/10.1080/13501763.2022.2141304.

Boli, J., & Thomas, G. M. (1999). Constructing World Culture: International Nongovernmental Organizations Since 1875. Stanford University Press.

Bosi, L., & Zamponi, L. (2015). Direct social actions and economic crises: The relationship between forms of action and socio-economic context in Italy. Partecipazione E Conflitto, 8(2), Article 2.

Bourgeron, T., & Geiger, S. (2022). (De-)assetizing pharmaceutical patents: Patent contestations behind a blockbuster drug. Economy and Society, 51(1), 23–45. https://doi.org/10.1080/03085147.2022.1987752.

Bracke, M. A. (2017). Feminism, the state, and the centrality of reproduction: Abortion struggles in 1970s Italy. Social History, 42(4), 524–546. https://doi.org/10.1080/03071022.2017.1368234.

Brooks, E., de Ruijter, A., Greer, S. L., & Rozenblum, S. (2023). EU health policy in the aftermath of COVID-19: Neofunctionalism and crisis-driven integration. *Journal of European Public Policy*, 30(4), 721–739. https://doi.org/10.1080/13501763.2022.2141301.

Brown, P. (2007). *Toxic Exposures: Contested Illnesses and the Environmental Health Movement*. Columbia University Press.

Brown, P., & Zavestoski, S. (2004). Social movements in health: An introduction. Sociology of Health and Illness, 26(6), 679–694. https://doi.org/10.1111/j.0141-9889.2004.00413.x.

Brown, P., Morello-Frosch, R., Zavestoski, S., & the Contested Illnesses Research Group (Eds.). (2012). Front matter. In *Contested Illnesses* (1st ed.). University of California Press; JSTOR. http://www.jstor.org/stable/10.1525/j.ctt7zw1q9.1.

Buckland Merrett, G. L., Kilkenny, C., & Reed, T. (2017). Civil society engagement in multi-stakeholder dialogue: A qualitative study exploring the opinions and perceptions of MeTA members. Journal of Pharmaceutical Policy and Practice, 10(1), 5. https://doi.org/10.1186/s40545-016-0096-0.

Cameron, E., & Berger, J. (2005). Patents and public health: Principle, politics and paradox: British Academy Law Lecture. In P. J. Marshall (Ed.), *Proceedings of the British Academy, Volume 131, 2004 Lectures*, pp. 331–369. British Academy. https://doi.org/10.5871/bacad/9780197263518.003.0012.

Carpiano, R. M., Callaghan, T., DiResta, R., et al. (2023). Confronting the evolution and expansion of anti-vaccine activism in the USA in the COVID-19 era. Lancet (London, England), 401(10380), 967–970. https://doi.org/10.1016/S0140-6736(23)00136-8.

Cassier, M. (2004). Brevets pharmaceutiques et santé publique en France: Opposition et dispositifs spécifiques d'appropriation des médicaments entre 1791 et 2004. Entreprises et histoire, 36(2), 29–47. https://doi.org/10.3917/eh.036.0029.

References

Cassier, M. (2014). Patents and Health. In The Wiley Blackwell Encyclopedia of Health, Illness, Behavior, and Society. Wiley-Blackwell. https://doi.org/10.1002/9781118410868.wbehibs355.

Chabrol, F., David, P.-M., & Krikorian, G. (2017). Rationing hepatitis C treatment in the context of austerity policies in France and Cameroon: A transnational perspective on the pharmaceuticalization of healthcare systems. Social Science & Medicine, 187, 243–250. https://doi.org/10.1016/j.socscimed.2017.03.059.

Chin, J. C., & Grossman, G. M. (1988). Intellectual property rights and north-south trade (Working Paper 2769). National Bureau of Economic Research. https://doi.org/10.3386/w2769.

Christou, S. (2022a). Health movements (Europe). In D. A. Snow, D. della Porta, D. McAdam, & B. Klandermans (Eds), *The Wiley-Blackwell Encyclopedia of Social and Political Movements* (pp. 1–7). John Wiley & Sons. https://doi.org/10.1002/9780470674871.wbespm569.

Christou, S. (2022b). The diffusion, modularisation and institutionalisation of direct social actions in healthcare. The Greek Healthcare Arena: 1983–2019. Scuola Normale Superiore.

Christou, S. (2024). Il diritto alla salute come master frame: Salute, sanità e cura nella pandemia. In D. della Porta, R. E. Chesta, D. Chironi, A. Felicetti, & S. Christou (Eds.), Comunicare e partecipare durante una pandemia (pp. 139–166). Il Mulino.

Christou, S., & della Porta, D. (2024). Contesting patents on Covid-19 vaccines in the EU: the No Profit on Pandemic campaign.

Collier, D., & Munck, G. L. (2017). Building blocks and methodological challenges: A framework for studying critical junctures (SSRN Scholarly Paper 3034920). https://papers.ssrn.com/abstract=3034920.

Corporate Europe Observatory. (2021a, May 7). The Commission's pharma echo chamber. https://corporateeurope.org/en/2021/05/commissions-pharma-echo-chamber.

Corporate Europe Observatory. (2021b, June 4). Leaked documents show EU Council of ministers defined its position on TRIPS waiver for vaccines in secret. https://corporateeurope.org/en/2021/06/leaked-documents-show-eu-council-ministers-defined-its-position-trips-waiver-vaccines.

Correa, C. M. (2006). Implications of bilateral free trade agreements on access to medicines. Bulletin of the World Health Organization, 84(5), 399–404.

Crespy, A., & Parks, L. (2017). The connection between parliamentary and extra-parliamentary opposition in the EU. From ACTA to the financial crisis. Journal of European Integration, 39, 1–15. https://doi.org/10.1080/07036337.2017.1309038.

Cross, S., Rho, Y., Reddy, H., et al. (2021). Who funded the research behind the Oxford-AstraZeneca COVID-19 vaccine? Approximating the funding to the University of Oxford for the research and development of the ChAdOx vaccine technology (p. 2021.04.08.21255103). medRxiv. https://doi.org/10.1101/2021.04.08.21255103.

Crossley, N. (2006). Contesting Psychiatry: Social Movements in Mental Health. Routledge.

Cueto, M., Brown, T. M., & Fee, E. (2019). The World Health Organization: A History. Cambridge University Press. https://doi.org/10.1017/9781108692878.

de Ruijter, A., Beetsma, R. M. W. J., Burgoon, B., Nicoli, F., & Vandenbroucke, F. (2020). *EU Solidarity and Policy in Fighting Infectious Diseases: State of Play, Obstacles, Citizen Preferences and Ways Forward* (SSRN Scholarly Paper No. 3570550). https://doi.org/10.2139/ssrn.3570550

della Porta, D. (2020). Protests as critical junctures: Some reflections towards a momentous approach to social movements. Social Movement Studies, 19 (5–6), 556–575. https://doi.org/10.1080/14742837.2018.1555458.

della Porta, D. (2022). Contentious Politics in Emergency Critical Junctures: Progressive Social Movements during the Pandemic. Cambridge University Press. www.cambridge.org/core/elements/contentious-politics-in-emergency-critical-junctures/1D03059F92DF5DDA9338D17F174E6D29.

della Porta, D. (2023). Regressive Movements in Times of Emergency: The Protests against Anti-Contagion Measures and Vaccination During the Covid-19 Pandemic. Oxford University Press. https://global.oup.com/academic/product/regressive-movements-in-times-of-emergency-9780198884309?cc=it&lang=en&.

della Porta, D., Chesta, R. E., Chironi, D., Christou, S., & Felicetti, A. (2024). Comunicare e partecipare durante una pandemia. Il Mulino.

della Porta, D., Kriesi H., & Rucht D. (eds). (1999). Social Movements in a Globalizing World. Palgrave Macmillan.

della Porta, D., & Lavizzari, A. (2022). Framing health and care: Legacies and innovation during the pandemic. Social Movement Studies, 23 (6), 738–755. https://doi.org/10.1080/14742837.2022.2134109.

della Porta, D., & Parks, L. (2018). Social movements, the European crisis, and EU political opportunities. Comparative European Politics, 16, 85–102. https://doi.org/10.1057/s41295-016-0074-6.

della Porta, D., Andretta, M., Mosca, L., & Reiter, H. (2006) Globalization from Below Transnational Activists and Protest Networks. University of Minnesota Press.

della Porta, D., Parks, L., & Portos, M. (2022). Environmentalism in Europe: Activism and advocacy. In T. Rayner, K. Szulecki, A. Jordan, & S. Oberthür (Eds.), Handbook on European Union Climate Change Policy and Politics (pp. 98–112). Edward Elgar.

della Porta D., & Tarrow S., G. (eds.) 2005. Transnational Protest and Global Activism. Rowman & Littlefield.

DNDi. (2020, October 12). DNDi statement on India and South Africa request to WTO to waive IP rules for COVID-19 health tools. https://dndi.org/statements/2020/dndi-statement-india-south-africa-request-wto-waive-ip-rules-covid-19-health-tools/.

Drahos, P. (1995). Global Property Rights in Information: The story of TRIPS at the GATT. Prometheus, 13(1), 6–19. https://doi.org/10.1080/08109029508629187.

Drahos, P. (2021). Public lies and public goods: Ten lessons from when patents and pandemics meet [Working Paper]. European University Institute. https://cadmus.eui.eu/handle/1814/71560.

Drugau-Constantin, A. L., & Anghel-Sienerth, A. K. (2022). Challenges of civic participation at EU level during Covid-19 pandemic: European citizens' initiative. Applied Research in Administrative Sciences, 3(1), 4–10.

Dyer, O. (2021). Covid-19: Countries are learning what others paid for vaccines. BMJ, 372, n281. https://doi.org/10.1136/bmj.n281.

Engels, F. (2009). The Condition of the Working Class in England—Paperback—Friedrich Engels, David McLellan—Oxford University Press (D. McLellan, Ed.). Oxford University Press. https://global.oup.com/ukhe/product/the-condition-of-the-working-class-in-england-9780199555888.

Epstein, S. (1996). Impure Science: AIDS, Activism, and the Politics of Knowledge. University of California Press.

Epstein, S. (2007). Chapter 21: Patient groups and health movements. In E. J. Hackett, O. Amsterdamska, M. E. Lynch, & J. Wajcman (Eds.), The Handbook of Science and Technology Studies (3rd ed., pp. 499–539). MIT Press.

Epstein, S. (2010). The strength of diverse ties *: Multiple hybridity in the politics of inclusion and difference in U.S. Biomedical research. In Social Movements and the Transformation of American Health Care. Oxford University Press. https://doi.org/10.1093/acprof:oso/9780195388299.003.0006.

European Citizens' Initiative. (n.d.). [Text]. Retrieved 2 May 2023, https://europa.eu/citizens-initiative/initiatives/details/2020/000005_en.

European Commission. (1998). European Commission (DG 1) note on the WHO's Revised Drug Strategy. www.cptech.org/ip/health/who/eurds98.html.

European Commission (2009) *Pharmaceutical Sector Inquiry: Final Report. Staff Working Paper Part 1*. Directorate-General for Competition. Available at: https://competition-policy.ec.europa.eu/system/files/2022-05/pharmaceutical_sector_inquiry_staff_working_paper_part1.pdf (accessed 3 September 2025).

European Commission. (2020). Von der Leyen [Text]. https://ec.europa.eu/commission/presscorner/detail/en/statement_20_741.

European Commission Competition Director-General. (2009). Pharmaceutical Sector Inquiry (pp. 1–533). European Commission.

European Parliament. (2020, December 23). Parliamentary question- Answer for question E-005595/20. www.europarl.europa.eu/doceo/document/E-9-2020-005595-ASW_EN.html.

European Parliament. (2023, March 31). European Citizens' Initiative | Fact Sheets on the European Union. www.europarl.europa.eu/factsheets/en/sheet/149/european-citizens-initiative.

f_barca. (2021, February 3). Covid vaccine contracts: EU has hands tied, experts say. Https://Voxeurop.Eu/En/. https://voxeurop.eu/en/covid-vaccine-contracts-eu-has-hands-tied-experts-say/.

Ferraz, O. L. M. (2021). Health as a Human Right: The Politics and Judicialisation of Health in Brazil. Cambridge University Press. https://doi.org/10.1017/9781108678605.

Gabble, R., & Kohler, J. C. (2014). To patent or not to patent? The case of Novartis' cancer drug Glivec in India. Globalization and Health, 10(1), 3. https://doi.org/10.1186/1744-8603-10-3.

Gaffney, A. (2018). To Heal Humankind: The Right to Health in History. Routledge.

Gaffney, A., & Muntaner, C. (2018). Austerity and Healthcare. In H. Waitzkin & The Working Group on Health Beyond Capitalism (Eds.), Health Care under the Knife- Moving beyond capitalism for our health (pp. 119–137). Monthly Review Express.

Galanti, C., & Christou, S. (forthcoming). Healthcare systems commodification between national and EU economic governance: Greece, Italy, and Romania between the economic and the Covid-19 crises. In V. Maccarrone & A. Bieler (Eds.), Critical Political Economy of the European Polycrisis. Edward Elgar.

Galanti, C., & Naughton, M. (2023). Using the unions: Healthcare struggles in Italy and Spain between trade unionism and self-organization. Partecipazione E Conflitto, 16(2), Article 2. https://doi.org/10.1285/i20356609v16i2p216.

Gamson, J. (1989). Silence, death and the invisible enemy: AIDS activism and social movement 'newness'. Social Problems, 36(4), 351–367.

Garattini, S. (2016). The European Medicines Agency is still too close to industry. BMJ, 353, i2412. https://doi.org/10.1136/bmj.i2412.

Gaudillière, J. (2008). How pharmaceuticals became patentable: The production and appropriation of drugs in the twentieth century. History and Technology, 24(2), 99–106. https://doi.org/10.1080/07341510701810906.

George, J., Sheshadri, R., & Grover, A. (2009). Intellectual property and Access to Medicines: Developments and civil society in India. In R. Reis, T. Jr. Veriano, & M. Cristina (Eds.), Intellectual Property Rights and Access to ARV Medicines: Civil Society Resistance in the Global South (pp. 82–110). ABIA.

Gøtzsche, P. C. (2018). Patients not patents: Drug research and development as a public enterprise. European Journal of Clinical Investigation, 48(2), e12875. https://doi.org/10.1111/eci.12875.

Graf, B. E. (1992). The politics of AIDS: An analysis of the AIDS Coalition to Unleash Power [University of Nevada]. https://digitalscholarship.unlv.edu/cgi/viewcontent.cgi?article=1204&context=rtds.

Greer, S. L., & Jarman, H. (2021). What is EU public health and why? Explaining the scope and organization of public health in the European Union. *Journal of Health Politics, Policy and Law*, 46(1), 23–47. https://doi.org/10.1215/03616878-8706591.

Greer, S. L., de Ruijter, A., & Brooks, E. (2021). The COVID-19 pandemic: Failing forward in public health. In M. Riddervold, J. Trondal, & A. Newsome (Eds.), The Palgrave Handbook of EU Crises (pp. 747–764). Springer International Publishing. https://doi.org/10.1007/978-3-030-51791-5_44.

Guy, M. (2023). COVID-19: An accelerating force for EU activity in health? In S. Börner & M. Seeleib-Kaiser (Eds.), *European Social Policy and the COVID-19 Pandemic: Challenges to National Welfare and EU Policy* (pp. 246–271). Oxford University Press. https://doi.org/10.1093/oso/9780197676189.003.0010.

Hamlin, C., & Jones, P. of E. H. C. (1998). Public Health and Social Justice in the Age of Chadwick: Britain, 1800–1854. Cambridge University Press.

Hassan, F., Yamey, G., & Abbasi, K. (2021). Profiteering from vaccine inequity: A crime against humanity? BMJ, 374, n2027. https://doi.org/10.1136/bmj.n2027.

Heywood, M. (2001). Debunking 'Conglomo-talk': A case study of the amicus curiae as an instrument for advocacy, investigation and mobilisation. Law, Democracy & Development, 5(2), Article 2. https://doi.org/10.4314/ldd.v5i2.

Heywood, M. (2003). Preventing mother-to-child HIV transmission in South Africa: Background, strategies and outcomes of the treatment action campaign case against the minister of health. South African Journal on Human Rights, 19(2), 278–315. https://doi.org/10.1080/19962126.2003.11865183.

Heywood, M. (2009). South Africa's treatment action campaign: Combining law and social mobilization to realize the right to health. Journal of Human Rights Practice, 1(1), 14–36. https://doi.org/10.1093/jhuman/hun006.

Hopewell, K. (2015). Multilateral trade governance as social field: Global civil society and the WTO. Review of International Political Economy, 22(6), 1128–1158.

IFPIA. (2021, March 22). IFPIA statement to European Commission.

IndustriALL Global Union. (2020, November 25). WTO members should ensure access to affordable medicines. IndustriALL. www.industriall-union.org/wto-members-should-ensure-access-to-affordable-medicines.

International Trade Union Confederation. (2021, March 1). Large expansion in vaccine production and equitable distribution are vital. www.ituc-csi.org/large-expansion-in-vaccine.

Iyengar, S., Tay-Teo, K., Vogler, S., et al. (2016). Prices, costs, and affordability of new medicines for Hepatitis C in 30 countries: An economic analysis. PLoS Medicine, 13(5), e1002032. https://doi.org/10.1371/journal.pmed.1002032.

Jenkins J. E. (2007). Baptism of fire: New Brunswick's public health movement and the 1918 influenza epidemic. *Canadian bulletin of medical history = Bulletin canadien d'histoire de la medecine*, 24(2), 317–342. https://doi.org/10.3138/cbmh.24.2.317.

Kaldor, M. (2003). Global Civil Society. An Answer to War. Polity Press.

Kapczynski, A. (2009). Harmonization and its discontents. California Law Review, 97, 1571–1650.

Keck, M., & Sikkink, K. (1998). Activists beyond Borders. Cornell University Press.

Light, D. W., & Lexchin, J. (2021). The costs of coronavirus vaccines and their pricing. Journal of the Royal Society of Medicine, 114(11), 502–504. https://doi.org/10.1177/01410768211053006.

Litsios, D. S. (2015). On the origin of primary health care. In Health For All: The Journey of Universal Health Coverage. Orient Blackswan. www.ncbi.nlm.nih.gov/books/NBK316278/.

Loff, B., & Heywood, M. (2002). Patents on drugs: Manufacturing scarcity or advancing health? The Journal of Law, Medicine & Ethics: A Journal of the American Society of Law, Medicine & Ethics, 30(4), 621–631. https://doi.org/10.1111/j.1748-720x.2002.tb00430.x.

Lopert, R., & Gleeson, D. (2013). The high price of 'free' trade: U.S. trade agreements and access to medicines. The Journal of Law, Medicine & Ethics, 41(1), 199–223. https://doi.org/10.1111/jlme.12014.

MacLeod, C. (1988). Inventing the Industrial Revolution: The English Patent System, 1660–1800. Cambridge University Press. https://doi.org/10.1017/CBO9780511522673.

Mahler, H. (1981). The meaning of 'health for all by the year 2000'. American Journal of Public Health, 106(1), 36–38. https://doi.org/10.2105/AJPH.2016.106136.

Malpani, R. (2007). All costs, no benefits: How TRIPS plus intellectual property rules in the US-Jordan FTA affect access to medicines (pp. 1–37) [Briefing Paper]. Oxfam International. https://policy-practice.oxfam.org/resources/all-costs-no-benefits-how-trips-plus-intellectual-property-rules-in-the-us-jord-114080/.

Maraboutaki, C. (2021). Gender and sexuality: The crime of rape in the Greek Penal Code. In D. Vaiou, G. Petraki, & M. Stratigaki (Eds.), Gender Violence- Violence against Women (pp. 25–36). Alexandria. https://alexandria-publ.gr/shop/emfili-via-via-kata-ton-ginekon/.

McKee, M., & Ruijter, A. de. (2024). The path to a European Health Union. *The Lancet Regional Health – Europe*, *36*, 1–6. https://doi.org/10.1016/j.lanepe.2023.100794.

Médecins Sans Frontières Access Campaign. (1999, December 2). Major U.S. policy change opens door for poor countries to produce affordable drugs. https://amp.msfaccess.org/major-us-policy-change-opens-door-poor-countries-produce-affordable-drugs.

Médecins Sans Frontières Access Campaign. (2020a). India and South Africa proposal for WTO waiver from intellectual property protections for COVID-19-related medical technologies- Briefing Document.

Médecins Sans Frontières Access Campaign. (2020b, October 7). Civil society to WTO members: Support India and South Africa's proposal for a waiver from IP protections for COVID-19 medical technologies | Médecins Sans Frontières Access Campaign. https://msfaccess.org/civil-society-wto-members-support-india-and-south-africas-proposal-waiver-ip-protections-covid-19.

Médecins Sans Frontières Access Campaign. (2020c, November 11). Governments must demand all coronavirus COVID-19 vaccine deals are made public. www.msf.org/governments-must-demand-all-coronavirus-covid-19-vaccine-deals-are-made-public.

Médecins Sans Frontières International. (2022, June 17). Lack of a real IP waiver on COVID-19 tools is a disappointing failure for people | MSF. Médecins Sans Frontières (MSF) International. www.msf.org/lack-real-ip-waiver-covid-19-tools-disappointing-failure-people.

Melucci, A. (1985). The symbolic challenge of contemporary movements. Social Research, 52(4), 789–816.

Mercer, M. A., Thompson, S. M., & de Araujo, R. M. (2014). The role of international NGOs in health systems strengthening: The case of Timor-Leste. International Journal of Health Services, 44(2), 323–335. https://doi.org/10.2190/HS.44.2.i.

Mowery, D. C., & Sampat, B. N. (2001). University patents and patent policy debates in the USA, 1925–1980. Industrial and Corporate Change, 10(3), 781–814.

Müller, H., Tömmel, I., Müller, H., & Tömmel, I. (Eds.). (2022). 311Strategic leadership: Ursula von der Leyen as President of the European Commission. In Women and Leadership in the European Union (pp. 311–330). Oxford University Press. https://doi.org/10.1093/oso/9780192896216.003.0017.

Murphy-Gregory, H. (2012). Rethinking the roles of non-governmental organisations at the World Trade Organization. https://figshare.utas.edu.au/articles/journal_contribution/Rethinking_the_roles_of_non-governmental_organisations_at_the_World_Trade_Organization/22892297/1.

Mylan, S., & Hardman, C. (2021). COVID-19, cults, and the anti-vax movement. The Lancet, 397(10280), 1181. https://doi.org/10.1016/S0140-6736(21)00443-8.

Narayan, R., Schuftan, C., Donegan, B., Narayan, T., & R, R. B. (2020). The people's health movement. In Oxford Research Encyclopedia of Global Public Health. https://doi.org/10.1093/acrefore/9780190632366.013.54.

Natsis, Y. (2017, September 27). Reflection Paper | BENELUXA: First results of multi-country cooperation on medicine price negotiations – EPHA. Https://Epha.Org/. https://epha.org/discussion-paper-beneluxa/.

Nattrass, N. (2015). Millennium development goal 6: AIDS and the international health agenda. Journal of Human Development and Capabilities, Taylor & Francis Journals, 15(2-3), 232–246.

Noh, J.-E. (2024). The fight for global health justice: The advocacy of international humanitarian and development NGOs during the COVID-19 pandemic. VOLUNTAS: International Journal of Voluntary and Nonprofit Organizations. https://doi.org/10.1007/s11266-023-00630-7.

Oxfam International. (2020, September 17). Small group of rich nations have bought up more than half the future supply of leading COVID-19 vaccine contenders. Oxfam International. www.oxfam.org/en/press-releases/small-group-rich-nations-have-bought-more-half-future-supply-leading-covid-19.

Oxfam International. (2022, June 17). WTO agrees a deal on patents for COVID vaccines—But campaigners say this is absolutely not the broad intellectual property waiver the world desperately needs. Oxfam International. www.oxfam.org/en/press-releases/wto-agrees-deal-patents-covid-vaccines-campaigners-say-absolutely-not-broad.

Peel, M., & Mancini, D. P. (2020, August 26). Covid-19 vaccine makers lobby EU for legal protection. *Financial Times*. https://www.ft.com/content/12f7da5b-92c8-4050-bcea-e726b75eef4d.

Peigné, M. (2021, November 4). EU vaccine negotiators: Who are the secret names dealing with pharma? Investigate Europe. www.investigate-europe.eu/en/posts/function URL() {[native code]}/posts/eu-vaccine-negotiators-who-are-the-secret-names-dealing-with-pharma.

People's Health Movement. (n.d.-a). Structure of PHM. Retrieved 2 August 2024, https://phmovement.org/structure-phm.

People's Health Movement. (n.d.-b). The India South Africa waiver proposal: Documents and commentary. People's Health Movement. Retrieved 28 April 2023, https://phmovement.org/the-india-south-africa-waiver-proposal/.

People's Health Movement. (2014). E.6: Struggles for health in Europe. In Global Health Watch (Vol. 4). www.ghwatch.org/sites/www.ghwatch.org/files/E6_0.pdf.

People's Health Movement, Oxfam International, Amnesty International, Health Action International, & etc. (2022, February 16). Civil Society Open Letter to the WTO Director General. www.twn.my/title2/health.info/2022/hi220204.htm.

People's Medicines Alliance. (n.d.). Who we are. People's Medicines. Retrieved 2 August 2024, https://peoplesmedicines.org/supporters/.

People's Medicines Alliance. (2022). A five point plan for a people's vaccine.

Pilling, D., Kuchler, H., & Mancini, D. P. (2021, November 30). The inside story of the Pfizer vaccine: 'A once-in-an-epoch windfall'. Financial Times. www.ft.com/content/0cea5e3f-d4c4-4ee2-961a-3aa150f388ec.

Pope, R. J., & Flanigan, S. T. (2013). Revolution for breakfast: Intersections of activism, service, and violence in the black panther party's community service programs. Social Justice Research, 26(4), 445–470. https://doi.org/10.1007/s11211-013-0197-8.

Progressive International. (2020, October 15). Dear WTO: Covid-19 Vaccine is a Global Public Good. Progressive International. https://progressive.international/blueprint/b6cf1166-724d-46de-884e-058f771562ff-covid-19-response-group-to-wto-ensure-equitable-and-affordable-access-to-all-covid-19-health-technologies/en.

Roffe, P., & Spennemann, C. (2006). The impact of FTAs on public health policies and TRIPS flexibilities. International Journal of Intellectual Property Management, 1(1/2), 75–93. https://doi.org/10.1504/IJIPM.2006.011023.

Rone, J. (2021). Contesting Austerity and Free Trade in the EU: Protest Diffusion in Complex Media and Political Arenas. Routledge. www.routle

dge.com/Contesting-Austerity-and-Free-Trade-in-the-EU-Protest-Diffusion-in-Complex-Media-and-Political-Arenas/Rone/p/book/9780367533465.

Safi, M. (2021, April 15). Oxford/AstraZeneca Covid vaccine research 'was 97% publicly funded'. The Guardian. www.theguardian.com/science/2021/apr/15/oxfordastrazeneca-covid-vaccine-research-was-97-publicly-funded.

Satre, L. J. (1982). After the match girls' strike: Bryant and May in the 1890s. Victorian Studies, 26(1), 7–31.

Sciacchitano, S., & Bartolazzi, A. (2021). Transparency in negotiation of European Union with big pharma on COVID-19 vaccines. Frontiers in Public Health, 9, 647955. https://doi.org/10.3389/fpubh.2021.647955.

Sell, S. K. (2003). Private Power, Public Law: The Globalization of Intellectual Property Rights. Cambridge University Press. https://doi.org/10.1017/CBO9780511491665.

Sell, S. K. (2007). TRIPS-Plus free trade agreements and access to medicines. Liverpool Law Review, 28(1), 41–75. https://doi.org/10.1007/s10991-007-9011-8.

Sellin, J. A. (2015). Does one size fit all? Patents, the right to health and access to medicines. Netherlands International Law Review, 62(3), 445–473. https://doi.org/10.1007/s40802-015-0047-5.

Shadlen, K. C., Sampat, B. N., & Kapczynski, A. (2020). Patents, trade and medicines: Past, present and future. Review of International Political Economy, 27(1), 75–97. https://doi.org/10.1080/09692290.2019.1624295.

Singer, M. (2009). Introduction to Syndemics: A Critical Systems Approach to Public and Community Health. John Wiley & Sons.

Smith, J., Pagnucco, R., & Romeril, W. (1994). Transnational social movement organisations in the global political arena. Voluntas: International Journal of Voluntary and Nonprofit Organizations, 5(2), 121–154. https://doi.org/10.1007/BF02353983.

Smith, J., Chatfield C., & Pagnucco, R. (eds). 1996. Solidarity beyond the State: The Dynamics of Transnational Social Movements. Syracuse University Press.

Son, K.-B., Lopert, R., Gleeson, D., & Lee, T.-J. (2018). Moderating the impact of patent linkage on access to medicines: Lessons from variations in South Korea, Australia, Canada, and the United States. Globalization and Health, 14(1), 101. https://doi.org/10.1186/s12992-018-0423-0.

Stafford, N. (2017). Sofosbuvir faces fresh patent challenge in Europe. BMJ (Clinical Research Ed.), 356, j1632. https://doi.org/10.1136/bmj.j1632.

Steffek, J. (2012). Awkward partners: NGOs and social movements at the WTO. In M. Daunton, A. Narlikar, & R. M. Stern (Eds.), The Oxford Handbook on

The World Trade Organization (pp. 301–319). Oxford University Press. https://doi.org/10.1093/oxfordhb/9780199586103.013.0015.

Stockdill, B. C. (2013). ACT UP (AIDS Coalition to Unleash Power). In D. A. Snow, D. Della Porta, Donatella, B. Klandermans, & D. McAdam (Eds.), The Wiley-Blackwell Encyclopedia of Social and Political Movements (p. wbespm223). Blackwell. https://doi.org/10.1002/9780470674871.wbespm223.

Swann, J. P. (1988). Academic Scientists and the Pharmaceutical Industry: Cooperative Research in Twentieth-Century America. Johns Hopkins University Press.

Szabó, I. G., Golden, D., & Erne, R. (2022). Why do some labour alliances succeed in politicizing Europe across borders? A comparison of the right2Water and fair transport European citizens' initiatives. JCMS: Journal of Common Market Studies, 60(3), 634–652. https://doi.org/10.1111/jcms.13279.

t Hoen, E. (2002). TRIPS, pharmaceutical patents, and access to essential medicines: A long way from Seattle to Doha. Chicago Journal of International Law, 3(1), 27–46. https://doi.org/10.4324/9781315254227.

t Hoen, E., Berger, J., Calmy, A., & Moon, S. (2011). Driving a decade of change: HIV/AIDS, patents and access to medicines for all. Journal of the International AIDS Society, 14, 15. https://doi.org/10.1186/1758-2652-14-15.

Tarrow, S. G., & McAdam, D. (2005). Scale shift in transnational contention. In D. della Porta & S. G. Tarrow (Eds.), Transnational Protest and Global Activism (pp. 121–149). Rowman & Littlefield.

Taylor, V., & Zald, M. (2013). Health movements (United States). In D. A. Snow, D. Della Porta, Donatella, B. Klandermans, & D. McAdam (Eds.), The Wiley-Blackwell Encyclopedia of Social and Political Movements (p. wbespm306). Blackwell. https://doi.org/10.1002/9780470674871.wbespm306.

Taylor, V., & Zald, M. N. (2010). Conclusion: The shape of collective action in the U.S. health sector. In Social Movements and the Transformation of American Health Care. Oxford University Press. https://doi.org/10.1093/acprof:oso/9780195388299.003.0018.

United Nations. (1948). Article 25, Universal Declaration of Human Rights. www.un.org/en/about-us/universal-declaration-of-human-rights.

Venizelos, G., & Trimithiotis, D. (2024). Analyzing pro-vax discourse during the pandemic: Techno scientism, elitism, anti-populism. The Communication Review. https://doi.org/10.1080/10714421.2024.2378576.

Waitzkin, H. (1981). The social origins of illness: A neglected history. International Journal of Health Services: Planning, Administration, Evaluation, 11(1), 77–103. https://doi.org/10.2190/5CDV-P4FE-Y6HN-JACD.

Webster, C. (2002). The National Health Service: A Political History. Oxford University Press.

Weisskircher, M. (2020). The European citizens' initiative: Mobilization strategies and consequences. Political Studies, 68(3), 797–815. https://doi.org/10.1177/0032321719859792.

WHO. (1948). Constitution of the World Health Organization. www.who.int/about/governance/constitution.

WHO Commission on Intellectual Property Rights, Innovation and Public Health. (2006). Public health, innovation and intellectual property rights. WHO. www.who.int/publications/i/item/9241563230.

Williams, M., & Ford, L. (1999). The World Trade Organisation, social movements and global environmental management. Environmental Politics, 8(1), 268–289. https://doi.org/10.1080/09644019908414447.

Winslow, C.-E. A. (1943). *The Conquest of Epidemic Disease: A Chapter in the History of Ideas*. Princeton University Press.

World Trade Organisation. (2020, December 9). WTO receives petition asking for universally accessible and affordable COVID-19 vaccines. www.wto.org/english/news_e/news20_e/trip_09dec20_e.h.

Cambridge Elements

Contentious Politics

David S. Meyer
University of California, Irvine

David S. Meyer is Professor of Sociology and Political Science at the University of California, Irvine. He has written extensively on social movements and public policy, mostly in the United States, and is a winner of the John D. McCarthy Award for Lifetime Achievement in the Scholarship of Social Movements and Collective Behavior.

Suzanne Staggenborg
University of Pittsburgh

Suzanne Staggenborg is Professor of Sociology at the University of Pittsburgh. She has studied organizational and political dynamics in a variety of social movements, including the women's movement and the environmental movement, and is a winner of the John D. McCarthy Award for Lifetime Achievement in the Scholarship of Social Movements and Collective Behavior.

About the Series

Cambridge Elements series in Contentious Politics provides an important opportunity to bridge research and communication about the politics of protest across disciplines and between the academy and a broader public. Our focus is on political engagement, disruption, and collective action that extends beyond the boundaries of conventional institutional politics. Social movements, revolutionary campaigns, organized reform efforts, and more or less spontaneous uprisings are the important and interesting developments that animate contemporary politics; we welcome studies and analyses that promote better understanding and dialogue.

Cambridge Elements

Contentious Politics

Elements in the Series

Black Networks Matter: The Role of Interracial Contact and Social Media in the 2020 Black Lives Matter Protests
Matthew David Simonson, Ray Block Jr, James N. Druckman, Katherine Ognyanova and David M. J. Lazer

Law, Mobilization, and Social Movements: How Many Masters?
Whitney K. Taylor and Sidney Tarrow

Have Repertoire, Will Travel: Nonviolence as Global Contentious Performance
Selina R. Gallo-Cruz

The Anarchist Turn in Twenty-First Century Leftwing Activism
John Markoff, Hillary Lazar, Benjamin S. Case and Daniel P. Burridge

Sixty Years of Visible Protest in the Disability Struggle for Equality, Justice, and Inclusion
David Pettinicchio

Aggrieved Labor Strikes Back: Inter-sectoral Labor Mobility, Conditionality, and Unrest under IMF Programs
Saliha Metinsoy

The Evolution of Authoritarianism and Contentious Action in Russia
Bogdan Mamaev

Relation-Building and Contained Radicalization in the Gaza Pullout Campaign
Eitan Y. Alimi

Protest Walls: Co-authoring Contentious Repertoires
Yao-Tai Li and Katherine Whitworth

Protest and Policy in the Iraq, Nuclear Freeze and Vietnam Peace Movements
David Cortright

The Contentious Politics of Global Health Movements: Contesting Patents in Pandemic Times
Donatella della Porta and Stella Christou

A full series listing is available at: www.cambridge.org/ECTP

Printed by Integrated Books International,
United States of America